CROSSING

TROUBLESOME

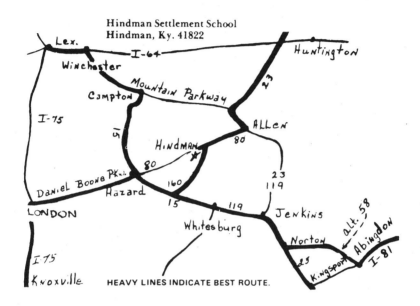

Hindman Settlement School
Hindman, Ky. 41822

HEAVY LINES INDICATE BEST ROUTE.

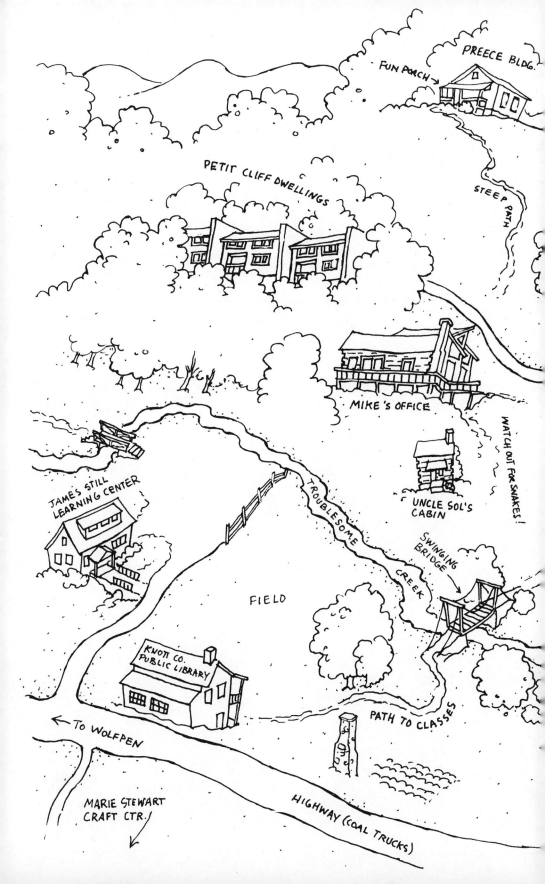

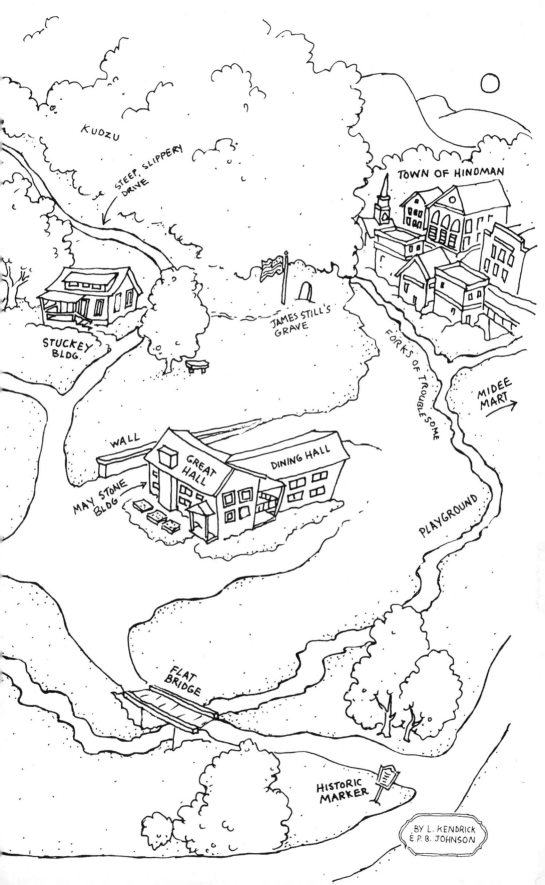

CROSSING
TROUBLESOME

---

25 Years of the
Appalachian
Writers Workshop

EDITED BY

LEATHA KENDRICK &

GEORGE ELLA LYON

WIND

Cover photograph by Sam Linkous
Map of campus conceived by Leatha Kendrick
and executed by Paul Brett Johnson.

While care has been taken to credit all photographers when known, we are
not certain who took a number of photographs in the archive at Hindman.
We are sorry if we left out any proper attribution of these photographs.
The opinions expressed are the authors' own and not that of the
Hindman Settlement School. All rights revert to the authors.

The poem, "Passage" from *The Holy Season, Walking in the Wild*,
by Albert Stewart, is reprinted by permission of Berea College Press.
The poem, "I Shall Go Singing" from *From the Mountain From the Valley,
New and Collected Poems* by James Still is reprinted by permission
of The University Press of Kentucky. The selection from the Jim Wayne
Miller poem "Harvest" is reprinted from *The Brier Poems* by permission of
Gnomon Press. The poem by Jonathan Greene, "Tobacco Love,"
first appeared in *Pine Mountain Sand & Gravel*. "Verna Mae's Braid"
by Laura Treacy Bentley first appeared in *Grab-a-Nickel*, Fall 1987.
"Songmaker: Metaphor for Rita" by Jim Hinsdale
first appeared in *Wind*, Fall 1998.

LIBRARY OF CONGRESS CONTROL NUMBER: 2002102687

ISBN: 1-893239-07-1

THIS BOOK IS DEDICATED TO

MIKE MULLINS

WHO FOR TWENTY-FIVE YEARS

HAS CONVENED US AS

A COMMUNITY

CONTENTS

{ILLUSTRATIONS FOLLOW PAGE 78}

EDITORS' FOREWORD

Those of us who have been at Hindman in August during the past twenty-five years know that something important has happened there. Something important has happened to many of us individually (as this book attests), and through that one-by-one transformation, something has happened to the region's literature as well. The goal of this book is to celebrate the part that the Appalachian Writers Workshop has played in a generation of writing—"generation" here referring both to the genesis of the writing and to the group of writers producing it during the past 25 years. Writers, known and unknown, have come to the Writers Workshop and found sustenance, community, inspiration and instruction.

Crossing Troublesome is not intended to be an anthology of miscellaneous writings, but rather it was conceived as an evocation of the Writers Workshop itself. Early on the idea came to us to arrange the book spatially and temporally, so that a reader might physically experience this gathering of writers in August. The text moves from crossing Troublesome Creek, to the dormitories, on to classes and meals, and then to the evening singing and outward to "Hindman Worldwide." Here you will find personal reminiscences mixed with tributes and vignettes. Along the way, some writers comment on the influence of the Writers Workshop on the body of Appalachian literature and the place of that literature on the world stage.

In order to preserve the unique feel of the workshop and its egalitarian spirit, we have included something by every one of the over 120 writers who sent us reflections on the week. This required us to edit all pieces, except poems, and some of the work was cut substantially. The large number of pieces necessitated other decisions as well. First of all, the table of contents contains only section titles. Because there are so many contributors, and because some of their works were divided and placed in more than one section, we chose to list authors and titles in an index rather than in the table of contents so that readers could quickly locate a particular person's work.

Secondly, we placed the authors' names at the end of their pieces rather than at the beginning, and we included the city and state where they now live. Our intent is both to show the broad reach of the Workshop and to allow readers to encounter each writer's words with the same shock of recognition or gasp of delight many of us have experienced at the Workshop's readings.

Assembling this book has been like putting together a crazy quilt— a merging of divergent voices, whose unexpected juxtapositions we hope will delight the reader, as they have us in the making.

L.K. & G.E.L.
MAY, 2002

PREFACE

I am often asked why there has been such an explosion of writing in Southern Appalachia in recent years. Why has the region, not known formerly for its literature, seen such a surge of new voices in fiction and poetry? Any time we witness such a phenomenal outpouring of an art we know there must be many causes, not just one simple explanation.

Yet I would hazard a guess that the example set by Harriette Arnow, Cratis Williams, James Still, Al Stewart, Jim Wayne Miller and others at the Appalachian Writers Workshop at Hindman from the 1970s on was one important source of inspiration for the present generation. Jim Wayne Miller was the first person I ever heard use the term "Appalachian writing." Through his essays and reviews, anthologies and lectures, and his own poems and stories, Jim helped launch the current renascence, even as he helped launch the careers of many young writers such as Rita Quillen, Dana Wildsmith, and Leatha Kendrick.

I am often asked what is the secret to the vitality of new writing in the South and the southern mountains. The glib answer is, "Because there ain't nothing else to do down here." But the truer explanations are in the great storytelling tradition we inherit, the love of language shown in pulpit, courtroom, storytelling festival, and the excitement of a culture discovering itself anew. For people in our region, history is real and present, and stories of history are real. And, yes, belief here is real. As with the Irish and African-American cultures, belief informs and inspires the Southern Appalachian storyteller, poet, singer. It is an advantage to come from a world that is not entirely secular.

It has been suggested that a culture becomes available for treatment in literature just as it is passing away. We can point to Hawthorne writing about Puritan New England once it has been replaced in the

American Revolution and the Industrial Revolution. Faulkner captures the old South forever just as it disappears in the 1930s. This may partly explain the current flowering of Southern Appalachian fiction and poetry. As the distinctive cultures of the mountains give way to television, shopping malls and super highways, condos and communities of retirees, the need and pleasure of capturing the voices, the details, the images and contradictions, become more intense, more relevant.

Some of us older writers still remember plowing with horses, cutting with crosscut saws, keeping milk and butter in the springhouse. But for the younger generation of writers such as Chris Holbrook, Silas House, and Stephen Marion, the past is the rapidly changing world of the 1970s and 1980s, post-Vietnam, a trailer park and K-Mart and media-saturated world. It is a world changing even as we look, even as we try to fix it exactly in phrase and image.

We writers owe an enormous debt to Mike Mullins for sustaining this workshop. It was Mike who kept Cratis Williams, Harriette Arnow, Jim Wayne Miller, and James Still, as well as Gurney Norman and Jeff Daniel Marion at the center of the Workshop. The gifts they have passed on to us are still bearing fruit every year, and still being passed on.

The Appalachian Writers Workshop at Hindman, held the first week of August every summer, is unique among writers conferences. It is affordable, open, democratic, and its mood is always celebratory. It is a conference where the beginner can mingle with the best-selling and prize-winning author. The coal miner and housewife can talk about their manuscripts with Lee Smith or Sharyn McCrumb. Writers of all ages and backgrounds can get advice about giving a reading from Barbara Smith and George Ella Lyon. For the writer who feels isolated in job or small town, Hindman is an opportunity to join the community of writers, editors, teachers. I know of no place more likely to inspire and encourage.

My favorite memories of Hindman are of the one-on-one meetings in late afternoon where both writer and teacher make a breakthrough in seeing how a poem or story might be improved, might be finished;

of Jim Wayne Miller laughing as he passes along another pun, found poem, malapropism, or blooper; of Jonathan Greene selling the books he designs and loves; and of the late-night songfests on the hill where we all listen to Betty Smith's angelic voice and dulcimer, and sing along with Rita Quillen and Cari Norris, Dana Wildsmith, George Ella Lyon and others, the old ballads and hymns of the region.

I have never felt more a part of something alive, a family of writers and readers, a community of writers discovering the culture they come from and the culture they are creating. I always leave Hindman a little exhausted by the intensity of the week, and inspired to be a better writer, teacher, a better person, and a better supporter of others.

The Appalachian Writers Workshop gives me confidence and hope and excitement about the future of our literature and our people. If we are lucky it will last another quarter of a century.

ROBERT MORGAN
Ithaca, NY

INTRODUCTION

The Hindman Settlement School's Appalachian Writers Workshop isn't your typical writers workshop. It is a gathering of kindred spirits who come together for a week of recharging their creative batteries. Of course, the craft of writing and the study of Appalachian literature are the reasons for the workshop but this is only a part of what happens during this week. Once you cross Troublesome Creek you enter another world and all the other things that you are are left on the other side of the creek. You are no longer a teacher, lawyer, doctor, etc. but a member of an extended family that are connected by the use of words to tell theirs and other peoples stories.

What makes the Appalachian Writers Workshop different? I believe one of the major things is the setting. The Hindman Settlement School sits at the forks of Troublesome Creek in Knott County, and it has been part of this community for 100 years. During this time, the Settlement has attracted a number of remarkable people who have felt compelled to write about their experiences. Beginning with the writings of folk poet Anne Cobb and novelist Lucy Furman, this literary tradition continued with James Still and Al Stewart, founder of the writers workshop. The writers workshop is an outgrowth of this literary tradition.

The first workshop was scheduled for the summer of 1977 with Harriette Arnow, Al Stewart, James Still, Billy Clark, Dean Cadle, and Shirley Williams on staff. The response was minimal. I arrived in December, 1977, and worked with Al Stewart on the next three or four workshops before I took over the entire administration of the week. The success of this gathering has depended largely on the willingness of the staff to work for far less than they usually would get. They quickly realized that there was something special about Hindman.

As we gather in the Great Hall of the May Stone Building for the beginning of the week, you can feel the excitement. The first thing I do is set the tone by emphasizing that this is a very egalitarian week and that there is only room for one prima donna on campus and that is me. I tell everyone about our rules especially about washing dishes and being respectful of their fellow participants. Most of this introduction is done tongue in cheek, including my warning about watching for snakes. I know that some of those first-time attendees are wondering why they are in such a place, but soon they realize that they are in one of the most supportive environments that they will ever find.

The Settlement's housing is limited so the number of participants for the week will never be more than 80-90 including staff. This number makes it possible to provide the type of personal attention that the workshop is noted for. When you have to live in close proximity to each other and share bathrooms with strangers there is a tendency to get to know your roommate or neighbor better than you normally would at other such gatherings. At the beginning of the week, the participants are slowly checking each other out and as the week proceeds you can see and feel them coming together as a community of writers. It is one of the most gratifying things to see this happen year after year.

Crossing Troublesome: 25 Years of the Appalachian Writers Workshop is a tribute to a number of extraordinary individuals. I want to personally mention those who are no longer with us. Without Al Stewart there would never have been an Appalachian Writers Workshop. James Still added a presence to this gathering that will never be duplicated. Harriette Arnow made the workshop a major priority even when she was too sick to be here. Cratis Williams promoted the workshop throughout the region. Jim Wayne Miller was the heart and soul of this week.

Hopefully, the magic will continue another 25 years.

MIKE MULLINS
Director, Hindman Settlement School,
Appalachian Writers Workshop

I

CROSSING OVER
TROUBLESOME

A Memory…
Troublesome Creek

sidles along
a Knotted path
its waters swelling
   then receding
with the coming up
   and going down
of this place
its bed silts
with the song
of this place
its bridge beckons
to the hill
then into the trees
hung heavy
with our words
of this place

PAM SEXTON
Lexington, Kentucky

———————

Hindman is a ladder
   a window
   a bridge

I am counting on the magic rubbing off on me

ANN TURNER
Hazard, Kentucky

I sometimes give this basic writing assignment: Describe a place using all your senses except sight. This turns out to be difficult for a lot of us visual twenty-first century Americans. Seeing is probably our most characteristic sense. It is the way we take in information, the way we check out the lay of the land and get a perspective. The other senses, I tell students, tend to create more intimacy: they are up-close; they happen between lovers and between parent and child. They come in through our noses, rub against our skin, make our mouths water. That's how I think of the Appalachian Writers Workshop at Hindman — with great sensual intimacy. I think of dense sticky air even in the early mornings when I took a run, and how the pervasive dark green seemed to fill my lungs from the hillsides, and the taste of breakfast meats. Mostly, though, Hindman resides in my memory as voices.

Even as I was driving into Kentucky, I was listening to the exhortations of radio preachers. As I drove away, I played tapes of Betty Smith singing, and they made me cry. All the voices of Kentucky and East Tennessee and North Carolina and Southwestern Virginia and West Virginia had a powerfully nostalgic effect on me, but what was remarkable was that the voices at the Workshop were talking about literature. That delighted me perhaps more than anything else: Lee Smith reading from her essay on Grundy, Silas House giving a talk on getting your first novel published, Jack Higgs digressing with a mini-lecture on the meaning of "Procrustean"— that these voices were both from my home region and about the intellectual adventure of literature.

The culture of the Appalachian Writers Workshop is at once thoroughly Appalachian and deeply literary. There is probably more respect for literature as a serious human endeavor here than at any other institution I've known. I think the reason is that Appalachians know that reading and storytelling and writing and speaking are all about the essential, deep, intimate connection created by human voices calling to one another across space and time through the spoken and written word.

MEREDITH SUE WILLIS
South Orange, NJ

It was a hot Sunday afternoon, my window fan rattling against the luggage in the back of the station wagon, when I abandoned the path most traveled and dropped the car off Highway 15 just south of Jackson about forty miles from Hindman, then followed KY 476 and Troublesome Creek deeper into the mountains, eventually past Dwarf and Rowdy, and finally alongside the now shallow Troublesome which would lead me to Hindman. I imagined the wagons of earlier travelers following this Troublesome creek-bed highway to the same destination. I had chosen this route in order to better immerse myself in the experience of a visit to the mountains. Though shorter as the crow flies, the route was, as I suspected from looking at the map, no bargain in time, though I judged it well worth the trouble of a few extra curves and minutes when I considered the scenery — swinging bridges over greenish-gray water, the lush and wilted green of late summer foliage, ironweed tall along the sandy creek bank, everywhere the threat of kudzu — and always the anticipation of what's around the next curve, and plenty of curves. And how many can say they've had the privilege of touring beautiful downtown Dwarf and Rowdy?

CHARLIE HUGHES
Nicholasville, KY

There's no one in charge at Hindman. That's what I like about it. Oh, Mike Mullins keeps everything running behind the scenes and occasionally offers up an introduction when we need one, but categories are slippery here. I was asked to be "on staff" at the 22nd Annual Appalachian Writers Workshop. I wasn't a writer-in-residence, exactly, or a teacher only, or someone else's assistant — and yet I slipped into all these roles, and so many others, during that week in Hindman, Kentucky.

I like the map of key roads leading into Hindman that Mike uses on the back of his annual brochure. It's hand-drawn and makes Hindman look like the hub of the universe. Which in some ways, of course, it really is to those of us who have been here. There are the spokes swirling around it: Huntington, Abingdon, Knoxville, Berea, Lexington. Labeled are I-75, I-64, I-81, 23, 80, 119, 160. But the most wonderful thing about the map is the small note Mike has appended at the bottom: "Heavy Lines Indicate Best Route." Only someone with far better eyes than mine could possibly determine which lines are truly the heavy ones, which the light.

I like that image, somehow. It's perfect for Hindman. There are no "heavy ones" at this place, no "best." At least not as far as I could ever determine. I've done a few things with my writing, but I'm hardly famous. Yet I got to eat scrambled eggs in the morning with Robert Morgan, who was just about to take the world by surprise with *Gap Creek*. He never brushed me away. My roots in the region are outmigrant roots (my West Virginia and Pennsylvania relatives settled in Akron, Ohio — Rubber Town), but neither participants nor staff ever reminded me of this or made me feel like an outsider. Not for a moment.

I taught a creative nonfiction class in the morning, but my "students" were published poets, journalists, magazine editors, people with life experiences so painful, so profound, that the stories they told and read in class sometimes made silence my only acceptable — only possible —

response. Once I was overcome with humility when George Ella Lyon and Jeff Daniel Marion visited my class — sat in the back — and just listened. I wanted to ask them to stand, and *please* switch places with me, but I quickly sensed this would not have been what *they* wanted at all. They wanted to be *participants* at that moment. Later in the day, or in the week, they might slide a piece of chalk between their fingers, or stand at a podium some evening and read from their work, but not right now.

In the conferences I held with participants, I was more often informed by *them* than they possibly could have been by me. I started routinely taking Kleenex in my purse when I met with them, because I knew they were bound to move me. Their stories hit my nerves. And they were *writers* writing them. Some were working on books and poems closer to publication — to real beauty — than my own. I followed their projects for months, often years, after our time together had ended. Many have remained friends, and the truth is that I can hardly wait to see them again when I return, "on staff," for the 25th Annual Appalachian Writers Workshop.

JOYCE DYER
Hiram, OH

—————

My first visit to Hindman was like attending a reunion with family I did not know I had until I crossed the bridge over Troublesome Creek. Hindman is a true community, and like all true communities the presence of the dead as well as the living is acknowledged and honored.

RON RASH
Clemson, SC

—————

Hindman—The Crossing

I arrived early at the settlement school, missing the entrance that first time. When I finally drove down the road, I stopped abruptly at the edge of what I learned was Troublesome Creek and stared. There spanned a rickety looking wooden bridge that had spaces between the road slats. What in the world was that? I had driven three and a half hours, and had practically cut off an arm in order to get to this writers workshop. Was I really supposed to drive over the bridge? Was it for decoration only? No, there were cars on the other side. I looked behind me. The way I came was too steep and narrow to turn around and go back. This is what God means when you are asked to have faith. I drove across, holding my breath and praying.

George Ella Lyon had urged me to attend the week long "Appalachian Writers Workshop." I managed to eke out two days, talking my mother-in-law into keeping my son overnight and promising to return home by mid-afternoon the next day, Monday. I found Mike Mullins, director of the settlement school, in his office. He was expecting me. I apologized for not being able to spend the whole week.

He told me not to worry. We take "good care" of people around here, he said. For several hours I watched a steady stream of people arrive, hugging and kissing each other like kinfolk at a church homecoming. Mike had his son take people's luggage to their assigned cabins like they were relatives. I slipped in with the group and ate a supper of corn bread and soup beans, a dish I had never heard of before.

Afterwards, we all went into the auditorium of the May Stone building for the opening ceremony with introductions of the teachers, including the "dean" of the workshop, James Still. I had no idea who he was. As I listened to Mike go over some of the rules, I was aware that I was one of a few without a mountain accent and the only person of color in this tight group of writers pearled and knit together.

[By the end of my first classes on Monday,] a veil [had] lifted and I could see fresh stories taking shape in my head…. There was so much to learn, I did not want to leave. I could have lain down in the grass on that hillside and drunk the cool mountain mist that hung in the evergreen trees. I had mustered up the courage to share some of my writing exercises in class. In so doing, I had picked up several new friends. I remember bunching up with people and staying through the late afternoon to hear participants reading and to eat supper in that place of words. I felt like an electron in a molecule, part of a whole, drawn in and spinning together. I ate quickly and as I got up to leave, people followed me with hugs and phone numbers and addresses.

I went back home across that bridge, but I wasn't the same.

MARIE BRADBY
Louisville, KY

———

Come August

I would be in Hindman for the gathering
of the clan of poets, Hindman my
birthplace as a writer. There Jeff
Daniel Marion first called my mundane
words a poem, and George Ella Lyon asked
"just whose story are you telling?"
a gentle effort to curtail characters
popping up in my fiction like summer
mushrooms. There I dried dishes while
Jim Wayne Miller talked about my poem
in Grab-a-Nickel — shitepoke, a word I'd used,

a name he'd once been called; I sat at
table with James Still and Verna Mae Slone,
sages of the word, written or spoken.

I would sit on the porch at Stuckey
where voices murmur of hopes, fears,
secrets, confessions. The house,
the porch, hallowed by all who've
gone before, their vestiges lingering.

I would see the morning fog, ease
into its peace, me someotherwhere,
the world a distant rumor.

I would hear words others have written,
my words rising to sing with theirs;
the music, morning song and evening
song, poetry and laughter; the rush
or trickle of Troublesome where the
muse bathes early mornings, wooden
bridge festooned with spiders' orbs.

I would wonder at words, like hummingbirds
in the rose-of-Sharon, flashes of ruby
and emerald, iridescent wings sometimes
hovering, sometimes taking the tiniest bird
on mystical voyages to domains faraway.

ELIZABETH HOWARD
Crossville, TN

Crossing over Troublesome

The sum of all our exploring is to come
back to our beginnings and
know it for the first time. — T. S. Eliot

In July of 1995, the moment I drive onto Troublesome Creek's bridge I remember running barefoot on such a bridge in Bell County, Kentucky. Instead of a settlement school, coal company houses line the banks of Cow Branch and our kitchen calendar says 1953. Daddy mines coal from deep inside the earth while Mother manages the camp's commissary. Our drinking water smells of sulfur and turns our bathtub orange. My sister and I "play like" the queen is coming as we cook and clean, and the mountains seem to fold themselves around us. Somehow, we close our ears to the coal trucks rumbling out of our holler as empty ones clatter toward thundering tipples.

I park my car and I am certain of only two things: I've come home and I must learn how to write....

Since that first writer's conference at Hindman, I've written two novels and have had several short stories and essays published. To see my work in print is wonderful, but it's the people I've met who have made my life rich and full.

Many, many reasons to be forever thankful that I traveled that narrow Kentucky road to Hindman Settlement School, crossed over Troublesome, and began the journey.

CAROL GUTHRIE HEILMAN
Irmo, SC

———————

A Bridge
(for Theodosia Wells Barrett)

In morning's fresh light we found a child
at the bridge.
>She greeted us,
"Teachers and poets are walking by."

I had labored for months with words for a worthy tribute.
>Here was my answer.
I had found in recent years a bridge from my
>past to my future,
and in the crossing I had discovered a noble
>example in a friend
who personified many admirable qualities I respected.
>Among them were courage, integrity, intellect,
character, compassion, perseverance exemplified.
>All represented a life of achievement and fulfillment.

I may never cross her bridge, but in my journey
>I'll remember what I'd like it to be.
I hear her voice, I see her yet on these paths
>and in evening shadows where we shared memories.
Thank you, Theodosia, for providing a bridge for
>me to follow, and for filling a span in
my time from the past to now to after.
In truth a teacher and a poet walked by.

AN ADMIRER

LOU RICHARDS
Kingsport, TN

Addie Davis slowed before crossing the bridge leading to the workshop. She spoke in hushed tones.... "The bridge spanning Troublesome Creek is your passage to a week unlike any you've ever known."

I was apprehensive as I followed Addie into the dining hall. The noise! I felt I'd entered into an old-time revival. Outside of church, I'd never witnessed so much hugging. Tears mingled with smiles.

Addie was talking to a striking blond woman, who flashed a brilliant smile as I approached.

"Hazel," Addie said, "Meet Lee Smith."

I suppose I stared.

Addie continued, "Hazel lives in Russell County."

During the drive to Hindman, I'd conveyed to West Virginia born Addie that Grundy native Lee Smith was Southwest Virginia's claim to fame in the literary world. "You know, Addie," I'd mused, "Russell County borders Buchanan County. Lee was probably born in the Clinch Valley Clinic same as I. We traveled the same roads. As a teenager, I'll bet she, like I, hung out at the Hilltop in Doran and swooned as Elvis sang his way from Germany to Hawaii on the big screen at the Flanary Theatre in Richlands."

"Well," Lee said as she hugged me. "Hello, neighbor!"

HAZEL HALE BOSTIC
Swords Creek, Virginia

Troublesome Creek

That was the summer my wife started speaking
      only by phone
      and long silences in the breakfast room.

When I came to Hindman,
      I was one of those things that go
      bump in the night, a wordless poem.

God was a cipher for my angry women —
      my mother, my colleagues, my new un-wife —
      and I was no longer going to his church,

not at Hindman, not at home,
      not in America, land of the free and blameless,
      of Presidents with easy consciences.

It was all those middle-aged school-teachers
      in embroidered blouses and denim jumpers
      who said, *Don't stop,* without saying it.

Gray-haired women, every one wearing glasses,
      said, *The creek is still running,*
      Drink all of it. Don't stop.

STEVE RHODES
Berea, KY

There was a heavy rain, and the roads were threatening to flood last summer (2001) on my first visit to Hindman. Everywhere I had met with Appalachian writers the past five years I'd heard how special the Appalachian Writers Workshop was. When I turned down the steep drive over Troublesome Creek I was relieved to complete the journey, but a little apprehensive. Writers can be friendly or not friendly, although Appalachian writers I've found to be mostly the former. I pulled in and three women on the porch walked out to give me directions for parking and lead me to Mike's beautiful log office.

Every encounter that week was shaded with this spirit of helpfulness, kindness, listening and sharing. The campus wedged deep between two mountains is tiny; its buildings evoke a noble history — such a small place with such a large heart.

SALLIE PAGE
Lynn, NC

II

ARRIVAL

from Finding Home

I had never driven across the West Virginia state line before, and a part of me felt like I'd just fall into an abyss, never to be seen again. Or even worse, I'd arrive at the Appalachian Writers Workshop and it would turn out to be like other conferences where the "real" authors and veteran attendees walked around having writerly conversations. I'd be the kindergartner, trying to break into a "fifth-grade only" game of Red Rover.

But Hindman was different. Within the first couple of hours, twenty people had smiled or talked to me, and my roommate and I knew all about each other's lives. I called home and told my husband, "For the first time in my life, I feel like I am home. There are others like me in the world."

CHERYL WARE
Elkins, West Virginia

I first attended the Appalachian Writers Workshop in 1993. Mike Mullins himself picked me up at the Lexington airport, which meant a very long drive on his part. I was flattered by Mike's attention, but the reality of his decision to retrieve me personally was quite different.

He later told me that after reading my work, he wanted to give himself plenty of time to make sure I was not some renegade outlaw who deserved no more than a plane ticket on the next flight heading west. I passed the test. We became good buddies because Mike let me stay. He even invited me back.

Many people attend the Appalachian Writers Workshop for the opportunity to meet and converse with a favorite writer. I must admit I am no exception. I went to meet a personal hero and literary mentor — Mr. James Still. Giving a reading with Mr. Still in the audience was a great thrill for me.

After that, however, I remember nothing due to a severe affliction of sworping.

CHRIS OFFUTT
Iowa City, IA

Gathering at the Forks

As I walked into Mike Mullins' office at the Hindman Settlement School I thought, "What have I gotten myself into? All of these college professors and teachers will make mincemeat out of me." As I registered for the writer's workshop I felt as if I were six again on the day of the first fire drill. I had missed the day of instruction. While everyone else filed out the door in an orderly fashion, I ran into the cloakroom to gather up my new book satchel and lunch box to save them from the flames. I rushed out the door and fell headlong down the concrete steps, cutting my leg and leaving a deep scar. "This will be worse," I thought. "This will scar my very being if I make a fool of myself in front of all these writers."

The next morning I breathed deeply and tried to relax as the old dinner bell clanged, gathering us for breakfast. After we filed into the lunchroom, we had prayer.

Soon everyone was laughing and talking in a language I had grown up with. I heard words and expressions that I hadn't heard for years since my parents' deaths. It made me feel at home. The group of writers had come from all over the country back home to their roots. It didn't take me long to realize that everyone was just like me. They were there to learn and share their stories. If I made a big blunder and used a word out of context they weren't going to laugh at me.

BARBARA DYE BARRON
Eubanks, KY

The lady who took care of me when I was a child would have said it was the Devil trying to keep me from Hindman that first year. I don't know if it was the Devil himself or his cyber minions from whom I got directions working, but something truly dark turned what was to be a four hour ride from Asheville, NC, to Hindman into a twelve hour pilgrimage through five states. In Bluefield, West Virginia I called Mike Mullins, got illuminated, and headed back south. Somewhere on a highway in western Virginia I passed a mobile home and a yard which haunted me with its familiarity. I pulled off on the side of the road, cried over my tormented vision and what I suspicioned to be the loss of my mind, and then realized I was circling back through country I had traveled hours before.

Too far lost to stop, I continued on into the night and the mountains. Arriving at last in the parking lot of the Settlement School and seeing the black outlines of the ridges against the sky I could tell only that I was somewhere deep within. The mountains. An ancient safety. A place of grace and guidance.

A white-bearded stranger appeared at my widow. "So, you are the Lost One?"

"Yes. Yes."

The next morning I crawled out of my little stall-bed, took a bath and followed a group into the dining hall for breakfast. A woman with the sweetest face and voice I have ever known sang a prayer. I knew then that whatever tried to keep me from this place must have been a great evil, for here there were angels to sing to me and table full of sausage and biscuits. Here there were others whose speech rang with rhythms kin to those of my home in the Blue Ridge and true lovers of story. Over dishes later in the week Jane Hicks told me that Hindman is a power place.

"You get what you need here," she said.

What I needed and will always need is this place of restoration. To come home to recall and re-learn what it means to be Appalachian in voice, mind, soul, and humor. To have mountains whispering to me every word I write. To be a writer is to always, at some level, be wandering. Hindman is the place I circle back to, to find or be found.

BROOKE CARLTON
Clayton, NC

Muse Control (or Mom Goes to Camp)

The radio station set back in Huntington
faded out just beyond Prestonsburg,
so I clicked in a handy tape and
listened to Crosby, Stills and Nash tell me
they are "glad that I (or somebody) got it made."
Kept noticing how my foot pressed the
accelerator, automatically
to a shocking 65 miles per hour till,
fearing blue lights in my rear view mirror,
I finally put it in cruise control
muse control so I could wonder during
the last 25 miles with peace of mind.

Wonder about how sane would it be
in a place as familiar as home
I just visit sporadically.
Would what's-her-name make it back?
Where would Mike assign me to sleep and with whom?
Now that made me snicker out loud, traveling alone,
singing words to a song I thought I knew. Suddenly
I was there and wasn't quite ready.
Hadn't sorted the expectations into
realistic and forget it piles
on the empty seat beside me so that
when I parked the big childless van
I just opened the door and sat.

Swiveled my legs to stretch three-hour kinks
out of bad knees and hips. Slowly pulled my arms
above my tense knotted neck. I don't know.
I can't decide about what came next.
But I felt like a lumberjack waking
up in the woods, feeling the moist air heavy
in my lungs, going down easy and deep.
Feet planted firm, hands on hips
like I was that "Brawny" man on TV
It was the smell of cucumbers that
caught me up short, that smell I had reveled in
only yesterday as I peeled the cukes
all slick and sticky, picked that morning

from the leaning chicken wire, sliced them
thin as onion skin. (I was making one last thing
for the family — marinated cucumbers —
a treat while I was gone.) I pushed my hands
to my nose to see if the sticky were still there

and that is when I noticed out of the corner
of my eye the coil neat,
heaped behind the left front tire.
Now I know my kids won't believe
I did a standing broad jump to the hood,
well, maybe they might. The kitchen table
hasn't been the same since the mouse in the
silverware drawer incident. I might

have been there yet, sprawled like a huge
hood ornament trying not to burn from
the heat of the engine or slide off
either, sit lady-like besides.
As nature sees fit to do sometimes
for those hapless victims of startling
revelations, I watched him move on
like a worm I had seen on my sidewalk back home,
ambled, strolled, even, over to the grass.
And I swear, I know that thing turned
and laughed at me before heading
on down the bank of Troublesome Creek.

August 5, 1991

My kids called my visits to the workshop "Mom's Camp."

CHRISTIE ADAMS COOK
Wittensville, KY

The Legion of Edds

My all-time favorite writers' conference moment (aside from washing lunch dishes with Lee Smith, that celestial being) features (as you might expect) Me, getting off my all-time favorite one-liner. Here's the set-up:

Mike being away one steamy Hindman August afternoon, I, Jim Wayne Miller, Denise Giardina, and (I think) Robert Morgan are copping a few minutes of richly deserved r & r between workshops and readings and conferrings, lounging about in Mike's cozy air-conditioned office as though we own the place.

In comes a sweaty, sorta seedy-lookin' book salesman, who spots Jim Wayne right away, and rushes up and shakes his hand and says, "Oh, I know you, you're…Billy Edd!"— confusing him, obviously, with Billy Edd Wheeler, the other famous Kentucky writer with two first names.

"Uh, Jim," Jim Wayne corrects him gently.

"Right, right!" cries the enlightened salesman. "Jim Edd!"

"Yes," says I, stepping into the breach, "and this is Denise Edd… and this gentleman is Robert Edd…and I"— shaking the salesman's hand —"I am Ed Edd!"

Well, okay, you had to be there.

Ed McClanahan
Lexington, KY

The Hindman Welcome

As a transplanted Kentuckian forced by the Great Migration to grow up in Michigan, I have long felt cheated of my original culture. The Appalachian Writers Workshop at Hindman has given me, at last, a connectedness.

In 1951, Mother and Daddy sadly tied their few belongings under a tarpaulin on the back of a red GMC truck, plopped me and my baby brother on the seat between them and drove 26 hours north in continuous rain in search of a "better life"— namely a job. Michigan did not want the influx of Southerners (oh, how they ridiculed us), but we had no other place to go. So, we dug our heels in, worked hard — and stayed.

But I lived for the two-week summer vacations that allowed us to drive back to visit my grandparents in southeastern Kentucky. There, while my parents did grown-up things, my cousins and I caught crawdads in the Cumberland River or held tea parties with Mama Farley's gingerbread served on sycamore leaf plates. Then each evening, the relatives gathered to tell stories on themselves and each other. And for two glorious weeks each year, I laughed....

In my first meeting with Mike Mullins, he stated I was a "displaced hillbilly wanting to come home." His use of that particular noun momentarily rankled since it had often been tossed unkindly toward me in Michigan. But suddenly I smiled. Mike was right.

My next surprise came as I met my roommate, Debby Clark. As a pampered motivational speaker, I normally don't share space with anyone. But Debby's warm greeting provided a safe harbor for my weary spirit. In fact, listening to descriptions of her family gatherings, especially those with Aunt Zenna, was like reading a good book.

Any concern I'd had about becoming a student again was quickly dispelled by the genius of Dr. Jack Higgs as he defined the Appalachian culture through literature — and all accompanied by laughter reminiscent of the long-ago guffaws of my dad and uncles as they traded stories. Then Chris Holbrook, the soft-spoken short-story instructor, encouraged me to write about my Great Migration experience — something I had never thought as having merit.

At the end of the week, I went home with my notebook, head and soul filled.

I used to think I've come a long way from that rainy morning my family left our cloistering hills and headed to Michigan. After all, I've authored or co-authored 16 non-fiction books and have my own motivational speaking company, which allows me to gallivant around the world telling Kentucky stories. But without understanding all the components that make me who I am, I was lacking an important ingredient. Hindman provided that missing piece — and tossed in lasting friendships to boot.

SANDRA P. ALDRICH
Colorado Springs, CO

———

Gurney Norman's *Kinfolks* drew me to Hindman. I kept asking myself, could an author really be allowed to write about families like the ones in *Kinfolks* with Delmar and all of his problems? ...[Gurney's] book was my first dipperful of words, fresh and clear like a first drink of water in the morning....

My family thought I was insane because I had decided to go to Hindman for a week and be with people that I had never met. I will not forget the feeling of freedom...I was not a stranger. For the first time in my life I was one whole person....

KAYE BIRCHFIELD
Pine Ridge, KY

from Kin Folk

I'd heard about Hindman for many years. from both Bob Morgan and Jonathan Greene — how much fun the writers workshop was, how nice the people were, how different it was from other summer conferences, how much I'd enjoy it if I ever taught there. I must admit, I was dubious. The place name seemed somewhat unpromising: Hind Man, the Appalachian runt of the literary world? And would good faculty and students really go to steep remote Kentucky mining country for poetic instruction? And — most vexing of all — was I really an Appalachian writer who should be teaching there, having lived for decades far away from my native western North Carolina mountains?

Eventually, Mike Mullins did ask me to teach, in the summer of 1996. Driving onto campus for the first time didn't really ease my mind: it looked more like a summer camp than an actual school. And my first conversation with brother Mullins wasn't exactly Algonquin Round Table banter. And my after-drive shower in the hill apartment...well, let's just not talk about Hindman's water.

But it didn't take long for my misgivings, my residual Tar Heel snobbery, to evaporate. After a few meals with the friendly writerly congregation, after talking and laughing and listening to a little night music, I was quickly won over, and I knew that Bob and Jonathan were right.

I'd been to other writers conferences, including the hierarchical hell that was Bread Loaf, and I could tell that Hindman was nothing like that place. And I soon realized what the primary difference was: This gathering was in Appalachia. Almost all of its faculty and students and staff were mountain folk. They were aware that they were mountain folk; they were proud that they were mountain folk; and I started recovering my own dormant Appalachian-ness. I understood how these people talked, how they thought, and especially what they laughed at:

I felt like I had come home after an extended sojourn in a flat and foreign land.

MICHAEL MCFEE
Chapel Hill, NC

———————

Since I was born in Wallins Creek in Harlan County in 1930, my Eastern Kentucky was a coal camp with dilapidated company houses, outhouses, and cows and pigs roaming free. Men, including my father, grandfather, and uncles, slaved underground and came out looking like raccoons with faces black with coal dust except around their eyes! Women like my mother and aunts worked from early morning (I'm talking four a.m.) until late at night caring for their families and waging an endless war against the black dust on the furniture, the walls, and even in their children's nostrils.

There was little time for reading, even if books had been available. In the coal camps along Highway 38 where Mama grew up, school ended at eighth grade. I knew there must be a different world. I didn't know what it would be like exactly, but I knew where it was — Chicago. I had an Alden's catalog sent from the windy city that I pored over every day. Surely those beautifully dressed women and handsome men lived in such a place.

Little did I know then there was a place called Hindman, a place where people talked about books they had read, and shared their own words, music, and love of the mountains and mountain people. Here was the world I dreamed of — right in my own backyard.

LOU MARTIN
Albuquerque, NM

———————

The Workshop

"Is this the Hendman School?" I asked the woman walking toward me.

"Hindman School," she corrected. "Yes, it is." She pointed me toward the weathered building I had been looking at with doubt. It has a sort of barn-like door that looked as though a quick shove with a strong-man's shoulder would knock it down. Across the little bridge over the almost waterless branch I walked and entered that barn-like door into the office of Mike Mullins, the director of the school and various other things, including th Appalachian Writers Workshop. That was 1996, my first year and the Workshop's 18th. I have been attending each year since.

I was born and raised in the Appalachian hills of Virginia. I left in 1962, going first to New York, then Richmond, next Atlanta and now I live in Tampa. I know and love the hills....

I knew I was at home in Hindman when the people around me knew what step-ins and heifers were and when they talked about "err" conditioning and supper instead of dinner. That's what I say!

I will continue to attend the workshop as long as I can. I don't drive and you must drive to get to Hindman. I have been bugging people for rides from the Tri-Cities airport to Hindman and back to the airport for years. I'm sure they are sick of me by now, but I will keep on trying to get there. It is wonderful, it is a learning experience and it is home.

Vera Cline
Tampa, FL

———

⇛LANDMARK⇚
ALBERT STEWART

Passage

Always the wind in the tree
The stream in motion
The season with leaves
And blossoms blowing...

What gave you the notion
What was it told you
I could stay?

Couldn't you see
Didn't whatever grieves
With the wind in the tree
And the world flowing
Tell you

I was always going
Always on my way?

— ALBERT STEWART

A Song for Them

In the beginning we sat before their feet,
Mr. Still the poet's potentate, the storyteller's sage,
Al Stewart the saint of sassafras, red foxes, dragonflies.
The two of them not saying much,
Especially to each other,
Later both regaling us with small town tales,
Their love of strangeness, observation,
Their writing rife with wisdom,
The flick of a freckled fish,
The scowl of a captured moon,
And the satisfying warmth of simmering soup,

Both with hunger for the tucked-in joke,
The silly story, quick-rhymed riddle,
The stumbling of adolescent feet
In meadow grass, on graveled path,
Or in a first-draft poem,
James Still betraying his amusement
With a rare, sly smile,
From Albert a chuckle coming
From behind his wrinkled hand
Or in the last line of an otherwise profound poem.

This is how I loved them best,
Those friendly enemies,
Those bickering saints,
In the sparkle of their fading eyes,
In the lilt of their light-hearted songs.

BARBARA SMITH
Philippi, WV

The Walker in the Wild
(Hindman Writers Workshop — 2000)

He is bent and frail, and his gait is shuffling as he makes his way over the foot bridge across Troublesome Creek. But the blue gaze beneath the brim of his straw hat is clear and piercing, in a face improbably youthful for his years. He pauses and looks over the handrail at the mossy creek bank. I wonder at his intense scrutiny. Surely in the 80 or so years he's crossed this creek and walked over this patch of land in Southeastern Kentucky he's become intimately familiar with all of it.

But he is Albert Stewart and we know that he sees the natural world differently from most of us. Many of his poems are exquisite reflections of that vision. Several critics have agreed with Charles Boleyn, renowned Methodist minister and like Albert, a child of Hindman, who termed Albert a "mystic naturalist."

Albert's mother died when he was two and when he was five his father brought him to board at the Hindman Settlement School. There is a picture of him taken soon after he arrived, sporting one of the first of the hats he would rarely be seen without for the rest of his life. His older brother Sydney told Albert that their father hated to send Albert away, but felt that he had to get him away from his stepmother's ire.

In Lucy Furman, writer and housemother to the little boys at the Settlement, Albert finally found a substitute for the mother he'd lost. She loved Albert like a son and they remained close for the rest of her life. There are uncanny similarities between Albert's tales of his early years at Hindman and in the adventures of Jason, a character in Furman's "Mothering on Perilous." Albert denied that he was the inspiration for Jason, but he was quick to admit that it was Furman who inspired him to write.

Writers returning from morning sessions at the James Still Learning Center begin to pass over the bridge, some murmuring quiet greetings. Albert acknowledges them with a smile, sometimes with a jaunty salute. I wonder how many of them know that it was Albert who started the Workshop. I gesture to all the bustle around us. "How does it feel, Albert, to think that you started all this almost 25 years ago?" He shrugs and makes a face. "Oh hush," he says. "Let's go get some dinner before it's all gone." He shuffles off toward the dining room and I follow.

GENIE JACOBSON
Irvine, CA

To My Friend, This Elegy

Driving once into the sweep of Cumberland mountains
On a high rising day brightened like any other summer day with sun
    and mist drift
and long-ranging green,
Where the narrow mountain highway curved beyond an overlook
I saw two men standing at the intersection of an unpaved road.
They were old. Not young.
Plain and plainly dressed in farmers' garb.
Both wearing hats crushed and shaped hard by time.
And one of them was dancing.
Standing in place, dancing,
Clogging a jig,
Light of foot, rough shoes crackling the day around him like
    the beat of wings.

And the other there beside him clapping hands to air and sunlight
and memory struck bright by other times,
Summers, autumns, falling snow,
And they were laughing.

I did not know you then.
I know you now.
You were the sudden leap of joy I felt that day
In mountain green and clarity of light,
The happy feet,
The clapping hands,
The heart's quick tilt and certainty that
more than even this was surely mine.
Now I am silenced here,
Alone in the darkening of a day,
Knowing that all such uncommonness of grace
As this you could have brought,
All of it,
Is gone.

BETTY BISBEE
Lubbock, TX

Velvet Sack and Coffee Cup

This request for submissions opened up a velvet sack of memories for
me. Every time I thought about Hindman, the velvet sack grew bigger.
My five years of the "Hindman experience" presented me with oppor-
tunities and events that are unparalleled. I want to share a few from
the magic bag....

Barbara Smith (one of Hindman's great resources) arranged for me to meet and talk to Al Stewart at his home. I was elated. I grabbed a cup of coffee from the kitchen, and we were off.

That day is still so clear in my mind: driving up to the log home; Al walking out to greet us, that lock of white hair falling across his face; him reaching up to his peach tree and handing each of us the luscious, ripe fruit. We let the juices pour down our faces as we savored the sticky luxury. He took us into his home, a book-strewn wonder. That day was the start of a wonderful relationship I had with him. I treasure all the many letters (complete with poems and drawings) I received from him over the years. From his memories on Lucy Furman: "I spent the winter of my tenth year in Florida with her and read *The Lonesome Road* in manuscript as she wrote and worked on the novel for publication. She was pleased that I wanted to read it and liked it."

His reaction to an interview request: "Why would anyone want to do that?"

That plain white coffee cup with the green stripes that I inadvertently shoved under my car seat and took home with me (Sorry, Mike) has become my favorite. Each time I hold it in my hands, it warms me again and again to the wonderful magic of that morning, that promise, that one-of-a-kind place called Hindman.

ALLISON THORPE
Edmonton, KY

III

DORM DESPAIR

The Bear & I

When I saw the rooms I had my doubts about this week at Hindman. I had been assigned the smaller room with the single bed and the rest of the suite was to be occupied by two other fellows — people I had never met. I was dubious. At other writing conferences where I had led workshops I had been given private rooms, and they had been a needed sanctuary, a place to gather my thoughts and review the day's poems. I just didn't know if this arrangement was going to work out.

And then he ambled in. A bear of a man who thrust out his hand and said, "Hi, I'm Jack Higgs." I would later describe him to my wife as mix of Andy Griffith and the brilliant literary critic Northrop Frye. She couldn't quite get her head around that and I just chuckled and said, "I think you have to meet him to understand." In any case Jack Higgs, who I think knows absolutely everything about Appalachian literature, made those rooms a kind of homey front porch for the rest of the week. Several mornings I went bleary-eyed into the workshop because I had listened to his talk of novels and poems and people and places far into the night. It couldn't have been more fun if we'd been sitting around a fire listening to a bluetick choir.

MICHAEL CHITWOOD
Chapel Hill, NC

---

from Stories of the Leaf Writers

The only way to try to explain the annual Appalachian Writers Workshop at the Hindman Settlement School on the forks of Troublesome Creek is to tell the stories. In a short essay I could not possibly give an account of all the experiences I've had there as a student and a teacher, all the direct ways that my life and my writing has been inspired or changed, all the wonderful, funny, touching memories I have. My mind leaps around back and forth through time from my first trip in 1981 to last year, 2001, when my eighteen-year-old daughter accompanied me for the first time. "I never realized, Mom, I never imagined," she told me after one day at the workshop, "where you used to disappear to every August. This is so cool!"

My first year I stayed in the downstairs dorm under the dining hall. Harold and Harriette Arnow were staying in the little apartment just around the corner. Late one night, Cratis Williams just opened the door after a quick knock and walked in. We were sitting around in our nightgowns talking, and Cratis was initially flustered and embarrassed, explaining apologetically that he thought he was at the Arnow's apartment. Very shortly, however, his naturally mischievous nature took over, and he began to enjoy our teasing him about his "alleged mistake."

It was decided that a photo should be taken to commemorate the occasion, and so it was that there is a photograph somewhere of a smiling Cratis, wearing my bra on the outside of his clothes, standing between two lovely nightgown-clad ladies.

RITA QUILLEN
Gate City, VA

---

from Kin Folk

....Nobody at Hindman [put] on airs; everybody was kin, which meant that we were all unconditionally loved and yet subject to the sort of mischievousness that family members visit upon one another.

One summer I was having afternoon student conferences in my apartment, which happened to be the one under the assembly room/dining hall. I was sharing these charming basement quarters with Bob [Morgan] and Jonathan [Greene], as it happened: Bob, our resident literary eminence, got the room with a door, and Jonathan and I each had one of the single beds that took up part of the open living room area. I was well into some sort of profound commentary on the poems at hand, edifying the heck out of my student I'm sure, when Jonathan walked in (having left his Gnomon Press book table upstairs behind for a while), proceeded to lie down fully clothed and shod on the bed directly in front of us, and — without a word — began napping as if nothing at all out of the ordinary were going on elsewhere in the room. We looked at him for a few seconds, then looked at each other, then continued our conference as if nothing at all out of the ordinary were going on elsewhere in the room.

Family will indulge each other like that.

MICHAEL MCFEE
Chapel Hill, NC

————

On Rooming with Shirley Williams

Teaching at the Appalachian Writers Workshop in summer was an opportunity treasured....

[One year] my roommate, also a faculty member, was a person of amazing flavor and ability. We shared a little bedroom. Shirley was from the local mountains, but also a highly esteemed girl reporter in Louisville, Kentucky, and I think was teaching journalism.

She seemed very refined and brash, outgoing, part career girl and American Indian princess. Before sleep, we talked philosophy, Kentucky gossip, teaching adventures, private thoughts. I told jokingly of my tussle with insomnia, then usually fell asleep. One night at about four in the morning, she left the room for a glass of water. When she got back to the door, the lock had snapped shut, and she couldn't get in. She didn't knock, but stayed outside the rest of the night on a couch in the living room.

The next morning I was astonished at what had been her (a stranger really) zany concern and politeness. Sure enough, she'd slung a blanket over the little creaky couch, and endured the night. I asked why she'd stayed outside, and she said she hadn't wanted to wake me up, so I mightn't get back to sleep.

All of which sounds trivial now on the side of humorous excess. In my naiveté, it reminded me of my Kentucky family in Louisville. Whenever we had visitors for the night, we gave them our beds and slept on the floor. I know this is a universal practice in many lands.

But at the time, the episode somehow fitted Hindman's glamorous eccentricities — the versatile and offbeat faculty, the long history of the settlement community, my friend, James Still, a prime supporter.

JANE MAYHALL
New York, NY

Higgs 'n Gigglin'

If I were only twenty years older, I could get away with a lot more. I could wear a large hat flamboyant with nuts and pinecone decoration. My red vintage prom dress plumed with petticoats would seem commonplace at a gathering after lunch to hear Jack Higgs' presentation. Truth is I probably could get away with relishing such a fashionable statement at Hindman....

In contrast, my first impulse after sizing up the top bunk where I would sleep was to evacuate. My concern about lack of privacy was exacerbated by my first impression of my roommates, Jan Cummings and Judy Hensley, that we had nothing in common. Soon, we discovered we had all been married to doctors. One, like myself, was a nurse. Some people call me Hilda Jane so even our names chimed in harmony. We had so much in common that I wondered if Mike Mullins had paid off the CIA for a background check before grouping us together. If I saw one of them anywhere, we couldn't help but giggle. We would giggle ourselves to sleep.

Giggling is what it is all about. It's okay to giggle because I am Appalachian. That is why I wish I were twenty years older so I could giggle the rest of my life away with Jack Higgs. I love a man who can talk about archetypes on one hand and giggle himself silly on the other. If I were twenty years older, no one would think I was odd to love such a man from afar — at least not at Hindman where every one is in love with not only Jack Higgs but with each other.

HILDA DOWNER
Sugar Grove, NC

A Tote Bag and Sneakers

When I went to Hindman for the first time over a decade ago, I had no idea what to expect. I guess I thought accommodations would be something like those in a motel, or at least like those in a college dorm. I brought various changes of clothes in a big burgundy Pullman bag, a matching cosmetic bag and a lighted make-up mirror. Mike Mullins told me I would be staying in the "dorm."

There were no porters, and when I lugged my bags into the dorm, I stood speechless, staring into the big open area with berths that resembled the open spaces in a honeycomb. I knew I was ill prepared to survive my stay in the dorm.

Shortly other ladies came, and by the evening we were already bonding. We were all ages, from early twenties to probably late sixties, and we were soon a tight team, sitting up every evening sharing our writings with each other. For many of us, it was the first time we'd ever read our stories and poems. We laughed and cried together and supported each other as writers and friends. For many of us, our writing career and our awakening to who we really are began at Hindman in the dorm. And I realized that all I needed was a tote bag and sneakers — and my Hindman family.

MARY BOZEMAN HODGES
Jefferson City, TN

———

Hindman Treasures

I arrived at my first Hindman's Annual Appalachian Writers Workshop the summer of 2000, nervous and excited as a green college freshman — suitcase bulging on all sides dreading to possibly meet the unknown "roommate from hell." Mike Mullins must have sensed the earthquake going on inside of me and mercifully assigned me to Stuckey and my roommate turned out to be an angel, a.k.a. Laura Weddle.

Other than the water smelling like rotten eggs and tasting like something far worse, I found Stuckey to be a cozy and comfortable home away from home. Its braided rugs, rockers, and "grandma's house" aroma embraced me like an old friend upon settling in. Stuckey housed primarily veteran attendees, but each one made me feel welcome. Upon meeting the rest of the conference participants at the Sunday night supper, I recognized early on that I had but a glimpse of the intimate family of friends in this special place. I longed to be adopted by this extraordinary group....

Return trips to Hindman will find my suitcase less engorged, my briefcase somewhat less voluminous, and anxiety replaced with anticipation of seeing my newfound family of jewels in my treasured valley along Troublesome Creek.

KAREN OWEN ADAMS
London, KY

This osteoporosic, emphysemic, hearing impaired, visually challenged, mentally deficient, accident prone, allergy susceptible, seventy-six year old, seventy-six pound widow attended the 17th annual Writers Workshop in 1994. She resided in the domicile of the decrepit where she was regaled by, and contributed to, stories told by the debilitated. She would like to attend another writers conference and share more stories, but the insurmountable problem of steep inclines prevents her from doing so.

SUE PUFFENBARGER
Bridgewater, VA

The Hindman Challenge

As the registration deposit disappeared through the mail slot, my husband asked for the third time, "Are you sure you know what you're doing?"

Maybe not then, but after a map and anticipation shepherded me across the narrow bridge into a world colored green and the office of Mike Mullins, of course I knew. I belonged.

Even when Mike pointed to the steep incline and said, "You're up there," I knew I'd love it.

Judy Roth and Marianne Worthington were my roommates in a small room that reminded me of bygone camping days. Twenty or more of us lived in the cabin, gathering on the sunlit porch, trading stories and words of encouragement. The great room at the center of the cabin drew us together in late evening, when we talked about everything from metaphysics to how we got ideas for stories. Mary Hodges kept us in stitches with funny anecdotes about her life in Tennessee and it was the best when she played her guitar and we sang old songs and hymns.

In the Dining Hall we ate like truck drivers. Great meals of ham and eggs and bacon and biscuits and hot cakes, bowls of fruit and bins of southern chicken and fresh corn filled us and carried us through active days. Before each meal, we sang a song of thanksgiving. After each meal, those on clean up duty, cleaned up, just like home....

It was an expanded me who drove home. Not physically, for the trek up and down that steep hill took off any pounds I might have added, but inside, I was different.

I became a writer at Hindman. And I knew I would go back.

CAROL BRODTRICK
Huntington WV

—————

My first trip to Hindman in 1978 was a life changing experience. I'd enrolled questioning whether I'd last one hour or one day....

Thus the first Tuesday afternoon found me lying on my bottom bunk trying to decide if I should pack and head back home to Virginia ...and forget the entire experience. As I mulled over the decision, who should walk in but one of my five other roommates named Barbara Smith. That moment and that person...changed my life!

She sat down and began talking with me — where I was from and so on and soon I forgot about leaving as we were both walking to the library where we sweated out an afternoon novel session.

At first I was somewhat skeptical of Barbara when I found out she was from Yankee Territory — Wisconsin. Thus I was rather guarded about letting her into my heart and soul. That is, until I discovered that she has a very great humility for the Appalachian people and the culture. However, by that week's end, Barbara and I had reached some sort of bond that hasn't been broken to this day — some 23 years later! We've gotten to know each other personally and she's been an invaluable aid in my writing....

JOLENE MORGAN BOYER
Jeffersonville, IN

When the Appalachian Writers Workshop is in session, Hindman Settlement School is a place of story. Stories are being written or read or narrated whenever two or more people get together. I remember one story in particular that I was told — though I have forgotten the teller. When I first heard this story late one night in the upper cabin, I went to bed laughing and got up doing the same. I shared it with everyone I met that day at Hindman. It was one of the funniest narratives I had ever heard, though the narrator was serious enough in the telling. And why not? It concerned her mother's burial. The story she told me went something like this:

"My mother was a very short woman (not over 4'2"), so when she died she hardly filled the top half of the standard coffin we bought for her. We all said our good-byes to her at the funeral home and drove to the family burial plot. Like many of the burial grounds in Eastern Kentucky, ours is located at the top of a hill. But it is steeper than most, so high in fact that the hearse had to downshift gears about halfway up, giving a definite lurch as it did so. When the pallbearers had lowered my mother's coffin in place beside the dug grave, my youngest sister wanted say one last farewell, so someone obligingly opened the coffin for her. My sister looked in, shrieked, "She's gone! Mother's gone!" and fainted. My older sister went rushing over to see what was wrong. She too looked into the coffin and exclaimed, "She is gone! Mother's gone!" and fainted as well.

By this time my husband, who had figured out what had happened, was laughing so hard, he had to walk back down the hill to recover. It seems that when the hearse gave the lurch getting up the hill, Mother had slid to the bottom of her coffin. Two of the pall bearers reached inside and pulled her back to the top and the burial proceeded as scheduled — once we revived my sisters...."

The teller forbid me to use this marvelous piece of reality in my writing. And for a long time I obeyed her injunction. But this seems a good place to finally share it with a wider audience. I wish I could remember the name of the woman who told me this wonderful tale, but as I age I find that names first, then faces recede into an irretrievable past until only story remains.

M. KAY MILLER
Jackson, KY

[EDITOR'S NOTE: This story has passed into Hindman lore and has been the subject of at least one poem.]

On the Porch at Preece: Daybreak
(for Genie)

I wake to the smell of coffee and for an instant I'm surprised that my husband has been up before me to start the coffeepot. Then I remember: I'm at the Writers' School in the mountains in a cabin perched on the top of a steep hill. Cocooned in a lower bunk, I have worried all night about the air conditioner vent humming next to my bed. The cold air blowing over me has inflamed my arthritis and settled into my trick knee. I rise and hobble toward the coffee pot, then follow the voices out to the porch where I know the talk will be. I wonder if our conversation ever ended, recall how the muffled voices lulled me to sleep last night. Had there been a break in our story? Was I the only one that slept all night? What had I missed?

We are dressed in bedclothes and underwear; white terrycloth and cotton, flannel boxers and silky nightshirts. Some of us are wet from a morning shower, heads swaddled in bright towels. The cigarette smoke drifts up and hangs in the mist off the mountains. We drink the hot, thick coffee and greet each other as we emerge onto the porch, the talkers pausing in their stories a moment to whisper "good morning." We are leisurely and slow, laughing and telling our stories. We are mothers all, some who have left their children for this week, others whose children have already left them. We have been farmers, actresses, goatherds, and traders; basket weavers, dancers, teachers, and liars; nurses, woodworkers, lovers, and cynics. Before the breakfast bell calls us down the hill for the morning meal, we have talked ourselves dizzy.

"I like it way up here," one says. "It's so private."

MARIANNE WORTHINGTON
Williamsburg, KY

IV

GREAT HALL:
READINGS & SPEECHES

The Prima Donna of Hindman
(for Mike Mullins)

From the stage graced by greats, he says,
"There's only one prima donna here,"
As if oblivious to Webster's:
"1. A principle female singer in an
opera or concert organization.
2. An extremely sensitive, vain,
or undisciplined person."

Is he female? Not that I have heard.
Can he sing? Not that I have heard.
He can, though, dance, at least the waltz,
And as he does he smiles and talks,
Shedding grace he doesn't claim.
Oversensitive or vain? Not that I have seen.
Is he "undisciplined?" Such a question!

How, then, can he qualify?
Patton, they say, was a prima donna.
"Old Blood and Guts," though, had it easy
With only the German army to face.
When our leader lopes to the famous stage,
He faces a bigger challenge —
Maybe as many as a hundred writers.

Without helmet or ivory-handle pistols,
He stands behind a lectern and
Before a row of quilts instead of flags,
A veteran of many campaigns, and proclaims,
"There will be no other prima donnas before you."
In the silence before him
There is gratitude he might not believe.

JACK HIGGS
Johnson City, TN

---

from Things I've Learned at Hindman

If you're reading in the afternoon session, don't feel pressured to give the requested bio — Barbara Smith will make one up for you and it will be much more entertaining anyway.

KATHY J. COMBS
Houston, TX

Words & Music

One of the wonderful things about Hindman is the spectrum of talents and experts on hand at any given time. One summer in the mid 90's I was teaching the novel class, and trying to finish "The Ballad of Frankie Silver" for Dutton. It tells the true story of Frankie Silver, a young frontier girl hanged in Morganton, NC, in 1833 for the murder of her husband.

I knew that there WAS a ballad about Frankie Silver, but it had never been commercially recorded, and no one seemed to know it. The wonderful Kentucky scholar Loyal Jones, who is practically a library on the hoof, told me that he had a copy on an old reel to reel tape: the ballad sung a cappella by Bascomb Lamar Lunsford at Columbia University in the 1930's. Loyal made a cassette of the song and sent it to me. I took the tape with me to Hindman, and since my friend the North Carolina folk singer and author Betty Smith was there for Writers Week, I told her that the ballad of Frankie Silver had been located.

Betty didn't know the song, either, and as a ballad collector she wanted to hear it. "No problem!" I said. "I have the cassette in my car." Except that we couldn't locate a tape player on campus.

So we climbed into my car, put the cassette into the car stereo, and cruised around the back roads of Eastern Kentucky until Betty had heard the song enough times to have jotted down all the words and memorized the tune. That afternoon she picked out the melody on her guitar. It seemed a shame not to utilize this new-found treasure, so we hatched the idea of having Betty sing the ballad to preface my evening reading from the novel-in-progress. That night Betty began the session with "The Ballad of Frankie Silver." I told the audience that they might never be able to hear the ballad anywhere else because it is so obscure, and then I read a short passage from the book and sat down. The combination of the haunting song and the passage in Frankie

Silver's voice made a very effective presentation. It was one of the most poignant and satisfying readings I have ever done, and it seemed perfect for Hindman, where so many talents cross pollinate, and where all the arts seem to blend into one beautiful rainbow.

SHARYN MCCRUMB
Catawba, VA

Verna Mae's Braid

Feather-weighted waves of silver spray
spill
silk-spun angel hair
earthward.

Hairpin splinters float
considered and askew.

Eddying ripples whorl and
channel soft, weave one.

Twining cascade curves
lovingly low;

plaits filaments of forty-eight.

Raw silk...waist-deep.

LAURA TREACY BENTLEY
Huntington, WV

from Remembering Appalachian Writers Workshops

Vivid memories pop up from my workshop photo books. Mike Mullins, in bright red suspenders, making announcements in front of Verna Mae Slone's beautiful quilts; Barbara Smith using Pauletta Hansel's back to autograph a book; campus-wide sadness at the death of Carl D. Perkins during the 1984 workshop. Special also was getting acquainted with *Southern Living* writer/editor Dianne Young. I told her, "You should list Sharyn McCrumb's newest book in the 'Books about the South'" page (which was done a few months later).

In 1981, scholarly Cratis Williams introduced me to the beautiful flowers along the gravel drive. Even as a fledgling Appalachian student, I admired his deep knowledge of the Southern region.

During the early '80s, evening readings were sometimes held behind the May Stone Building with audiences occupying folding chairs and the stone wall. Even fellow students stretched our imaginations —Virgie Hortenstine's excellent reading manner gave me confidence to share my writings.

PATRICIA SHIRLEY
Knoxville, TN

On Reading at Hindman

At the University of Kentucky on April 4, [2002], before giving a reading of some of my works, I informed the audience that my being there to read marked only the second time in my long years of writing that I had agreed to read from my personal writings. That such was simply not my nature to do so. I also told them that this reading had come about much as had the first one: the urging of a long and real friend with a voice just this side of a death-wish — my old friend Gurney Norman, whom I had met at the Appalachian Writers Workshop many years ago when we were both members of the workshop staff. I told them that the first reading had been at the Appalachian Writers Workshop at Hindman where I was teaching the short story. I, having begun with it at its inception under the direction of Kentucky's great poet and friend Al Stewart at Morehead University, followed it to Pippa Passes and Alice Lloyd College, and then to its permanent location at Hindman where the untiring efforts and dedication of Mike Mullins had turned it from a regional workshop into one of national ranking. Yet, never, never, had I chosen to read from my own writings. Was certain I never would.

And may not have except for the coaxing voices of two great friends and fellow writers, Jim Still and Al Stewart, who had blown the importance of my reading far out of proportion, matching Gurney's death-wish request and then some.... And not only had they talked me into reading but had chosen what they hoped I would choose to read: a short story titled "Hallelujah Brother Brimstone." One of their all-time favorites — they claimed.

Now, I'm not saying that what happened at that reading had anything to do with the long in-between to my second reading. You can judge that for yourself. Judge how it turned out, too. Whichever, I'll pass on to you a habit Jim Still had of giving an audience the makings of a story and leaving them to write the ending. So be it.....

It was the custom then at the workshop to have a staff member read from his or her works after sundown, outside the dining hall. And far as readings were concerned, they had signed them all but me.... On the night of my reading, due to ominous clouds that spoke of the chance of rain (and, looking back, could have been a forewarning), my reading of "Hallelujah Brother Brimstone" was moved inside the dining hall. We hovered inside like a covey of quail, watching lightning from far off fingering the sky and moving closer. And as vivid to me as it was back then, the more I read the story, the closer the lightning became. Caught up in the reading, I failed to see the uneasiness that had come over the crowd. By the time I did notice, I saw that they had one eye on me and the other cast toward the large window that framed the front of the dining room.

Uneasy myself now, I hurried the reading to reach that moment where Brother Brimstone locked horns with Josh and Todd Bulswick. Outside, the sky had turned as black as the inside of a belly mine up Big Sandy. It was as if salvation for the lot of us was at stake.

And then it happened! A great bolt of lightning knocked out the electricity and lit up the room like a quivering glow of doom! Caught now between a promise and perhaps my own chance for repentance, I fought going on or stopping where I was. It did appear to me that the audience might have chosen the latter. The room was as silent as death. And then the lightning eased off like the flickering wick of a dying candle in a low wind and in doing so seemed to give some hope to us all; hope that we might just make it through the reading after all!

BILLY C. CLARK
Farmville, VA

Hindman Poetry Reading

An argyle sweater man in silver spectacles
sits shoulder-to-chin with a
pink linen lady in champagne hair.
They listen to me and nod,
smiles gathering, the corners of their eyes
frayed by years of leaning toward
one another.
They breathe in unison.
We will grow old like this:
no need for word or argument.
A settled peace will filter down like
sunlight on the windowsill.

PIA SEAGRAVE
Spotsylvania, VA

Signed Books

There is something special about a book signed at Hindman. The inscriptions reflect the personality of the author and bring to mind time spent with them.

Mr. Still often made comments about the books that he signed for me. I once asked him to personalize a small soft-cover book containing an early version of "The Nest." When I told him my name he chuckled and said, "Alice in Wonderland." That is what he wrote in the book. Each time I asked him to sign one of my three first edition copies of *River of Earth* he would say, "This is expensive, you ought to sell it."

Browsing through my bookshelves I find all sorts of inscriptions that remind me of Hindman. Among them I read, "at Hindman," "with fond memories of Hindman," "to a fellow Hindmanite," "at the forks of Troublesome," "to my Hindman friend," "glad to meet you at Hindman," "best wishes to a Cosmic Possum," "more mountain music," "from Alma's mountain top, these poems of strength and survival," "to my friend of song," "with great memories of Hindman," "for avid reader Alice," "with shared good memories," "to a fair and tender lady herself," "at Hindman, our other home."

A signed book is just the best thing in the world!

ALICE HALE ADAMS
Fordsville, KY

––––––––––

In 1978 I had a grant to distribute books, not only from my own press (Gnomon) but from many other small presses throughout the country. So when I was invited to sell books at the Highlands Festival in Abingdon, Virginia, I thought it my duty to set up a table and peddle my wares.

I realized soon after I accepted this invitation that the Appalachian Writers Workshop at Hindman was going on at the same time and I arranged to stop by there for lunch on my way to Virginia. After lunch a few participants asked if I had books with me and when I answered in the positive they followed me like the pied piper and quickly devoured some of my stock from the back of my station wagon.

That night I slept on Jack Wright's floor in Wise, Virginia. Jack was then head of June Appal Recordings, a part of Appalshop in Whitesburg. In the morning I hastened on to the Martha Washington Inn in Abingdon and introduced myself to Fred and Susan Chappell whom I spotted having breakfast. I set up my display. Danny Marion came by during a presentation by Doris Betts and bought one or two books. I hardly sold any more books that whole lonely day....

The result of that short time between lunch and classes at Hindman caused a little light to come on — to sell books Hindman was where I needed to be not Abingdon — and almost every year since I have made my way there to sell books, give talks about publishing, and once every lustrum or so read my poetry. Many authors I have published have been on staff, given readings, or participated in one way or another: Wendell Berry, Jo Carson, Chris Holbrook, Jane Wilson Joyce, Ed McClanahan, Michael McFee, Jim Wayne Miller, Robert Morgan, Gurney Norman, James Still (in alphabetical order). I also distribute a number of books by others who have been involved at Hindman one way or another: Albert Stewart and Cratis Williams, and Bobbie Ann Mason. Mike Mullins has always made me feel welcome, always found a bed for me somewhere; Hindman end of July/ early August has become a second home.

JONATHAN GREENE
Franklin County, KY

The Flood at Troublesome Creek 2001
or Listen to Mike

Mike Mullins welcomed all of us
July, Two-Thousand-One.
We met old friends, and some met new,
And contemplated what to do,
Then filled our hearts with mountain view.
The workshop had begun.

Mike taught us how to choose each class
And where to put our mark.
He told us where each class would meet,
And when to come, and where to eat.
We'd sing and make each night complete.
He told us where to park.

Consider now the parking rules.
Good reasons Mike did find
Out front was saved for guests and all
Who spoke succinctly in our hall,
And for deliveries, I recall.
And so we parked behind.

We learned and shared and were in awe
When speakers came and talked.
We looked at books and checked each stack.
We rocked out front and mused out back.
And then took notes from Doctor Jack.
By Troublesome we walked.

Good friends by Friday we had found.
Much more than when we started.
We'd shared each other's verse and prose.
A list of e-mails we composed.
And thus our workshop days were closed.
And most the group departed.

By Friday evening still a few
Had lingered on that night
Celeste and Cathy, Daisy, me;
We laughed and talked and sang off key.
And dodged the rain to some degree.
And knew not of our plight.

The storms and thunder could be heard
As we slept in the hall.
The creek exploded from its banks,
And we were victims of its pranks,
And owed a million, trillion thanks
When Jim Phelps came to call;

With bleary eyes, we switched the light
And saw that dripping fella.
"The creek has covered bridge and lawn.
Before the coming of the dawn,
Those cars out there might could be gone."
He left with his umbrella.

I grabbed a flashlight and my robe
And slogged into the night
The pole light lent a ghastly sheen
As Troublesome raged on between
My car and all that could be seen!
I clutched my keys in fright

The waters lapped at my front tires!
No sight was ever stranger.
I'll grab the wheel and gamely strive
To keep my little car alive.
"Shift to REVERSE, Jan. Don't shift DRIVE."
I backed out of the danger.

Now I recalled that Mike had said.
"Don't park out in those places."
But his advice I did not heed.
(I couldn't ascertain the need.)
From workshop rules we had been freed
With all those empty spaces.

But now his laws I *will* obey.
Explained to us and drawn us.
Two-Thousand-Two or later when
I come to drive these roads again.
UPHILL I'll park, or Mike will send
The wrath of God upon us!

JAN CUMMINS
Montgomery, TX

❧ LANDMARK ☙
JAMES STILL

I Shall Go Singing

Until the leaf of my face withers,
Until my veins are blue as flying geese,
And the mossed shingles of my voice clatter
In winter wind, I shall be young and have my say.
I shall have my say and sing my songs,
I shall give words to rain and tongues to stones,
And the child in me shall speak his turn,
And the old, old man rattle his bones.
Until my blood purples like castor bean stalks,
I shall go singing, my words like hawks.

— JAMES STILL

Bookmobile

Harnessed into his khakis and brogans,
his Arbuckle Sugar box packed
with scarce, treasured volumes,
James Still stepped out
to meet the sun-ball.
Shifting his load
from shoulder to shoulder,
he trudged unpaved traces,
followed creeks through dark coves,
climbed to the hollers' heads
and traded the unread
for the well read.
Man-mule, he tugged
new horizons to
those who lived
at their jagged edge.

JIM HINSDALE
Tryon, NC

———————

Finding Mr. Still at the Public Library

After falling off a ladder at my son's house in Knoxville, Tennessee, I spent one night in the hospital. Then a doctor handed me a prescription for pain and a pair of crutches and said, *Go home. Get some sleep.* Instead, I drive to the Public Library. A skinny book of poetry bounds from the shelf and into my hands. I sit down and read it cover to cover. Amazed, I get up, hobble on my new crutches to the librarian's desk, and ask her if she ever heard of James Still. I'll give you his address, she answers. Amazed for the second time, I leave the library feeling pretty lucky.

With address in hand, I return to Hartland, Wisconsin, write a letter to Mr. Still, and tell him how much I like his poetry. Then, read my novel, he answers. I do. To me, each sentence reads like a poem. I am amazed.

Next August, I drive to the Appalachian Writers Workshop at Hindman.

Coincidentally, hind means deer and so does hart. Hindman, Hartland: Deerman, Deerland. My friend, Kathy Miner, says there are no coincidences. We never stumble onto anything. Things are placed in our paths so that we find them. I tell Kathy how a book of poems fell into my hands.

I write a poem and submit it. It gets published in the 2002 Wisconsin Poets' Calendar. I fear Mr. Still will not like being called a man in cat's clothing, but I take a chance. Incidentally (not coincidentally) Mr. Still becomes my favorite poet.

ELAINE CAVANAUGH
Hartland, WI

Listening to James Still

With another workshop participant, I was sitting with Mr. Still at a table in the dining hall one afternoon, sunlight lengthening across the floor as, in answer to our questions, he talked about the Great Depression and about the work of John Steinbeck, Katherine Anne Porter and other writers some of whom, I knew from other reading, had also admired his work. I said I liked his poem, "On Being Drafted into the U.S. Army…" and asked if he might tell any of his experiences of World War II.

He recalled when he was just out of boot camp and was standing among hundreds of young recruits packed close together on the deck of a troop vessel as it departed New York City, late one night, for Europe, for the war. They betrayed no care for where they were bound. "We were boisterous," he told us. "Jesting and singing."

The night fog was so thick over the water that, when the ship moved out into the harbor, the buildings of the city blurred into "tall, ghostly blocks." All the men sang louder together, he said, singing songs as if in celebration.

Then, as the ship turned, the fog thinned and the Statue of Liberty rose into view. "We fell silent. Not a word between us." He glanced at us. "That was the first time I saw it."

We understood: In that moment, some feeling of what lay ahead, of what was at stake, had settled upon these men. And some would not be coming back.

His fierce, bright gaze, his sober, low tone of voice. One felt his understated, forceful presence alone as a kind of model for how to approach writing, the discipline of it, the precision it would require.

DAVID TODD
Silver Spring, MD

I became acquainted with Mr. Still when he came into the office supply and equipment store I owned in Hazard, Kentucky. I was a late comer to the writing business and was having little or no success in having my material read by publishers. One day when Mr. Still was in my office picking up typing paper and typewriter ribbons, I mentioned to him that I did not think publishers read anything that was sent to them. He looked around the office at the books and magazines and said, "Someone evidently is."

Those three words were a wake-up call to me. I began to attend every writers' workshop in the area, in order to not only learn and improve my writing, but to be able to talk to known writers and to others interested in writing as I was.

For several years I attended some of the evening readings by authors at the Appalachian Writers Workshop.... In 1996, I was at the school to attend Mr. Still's 90th birthday celebration. I had an opportunity to talk to him and was pleasantly surprised to find he remembered me and the discussion we had in my office several years before. By that time I had retired and closed my store and had not seen him for some time. After that day, I talked to Mr. Still regularly.

I had written several short stories and talked to The Jesse Stuart Foundation about having them published in book form. They agreed and the resulting book, *A Ride on a Train and Other Moving Stories,* was published in 1998.... I was fortunate in being able to read one of the short stories from the book, "The Turkey Raffle," at one of the afternoon participants' readings [at the 1999 Writers Workshop].

CHARLES B. SIMPSON
Hazard, KY

Witness

On Thursday evening I waited patiently in the main hall at Hindman to hear Mr. Still, the Kentucky legend, speak.... I had seen him for most of my stay at Hindman but never could approach him. Always he was surrounded by famous authors, others who knew and laid claim to him. Short of bodily removing one of these acolytes from their chair, which did flit through my mind on more than one occasion, there was nothing I could do but go to the lecture that evening. Maybe then I would glean something from this great artist. He struggled out of his rocker and shuffled unsteadily but continuously toward the stage. I heard a light whisper as he passed my row. "He won't be here long," it said. "You must talk with him tonight."

How could I possibly do that? I hadn't got anywhere near him all week and now the room was jam-packed full of people, many more than had attended the workshop. So I sat and listened and was generally well behaved until Mr. Still read aloud from [a story] about two women who were so dumb that they should have had their heads pinched off at birth. Tears rolled down my face as I tried to restrain my laughter, laughter that went on too long. After several poems Mr. Still stepped from the stage, swallowed up by the crowd.

"What was the name of that book?" I asked Jonathan Greene, standing behind his booksellers counter. "What book?" Mr. Still asked. He had materialized at my side, cane in hand.

"The one with the story. I want it."

"*Pattern of a Man,*" he said. I bought it and he was again absorbed into the crowd. Why was it so important that I see this man? What could he possibly impart to me personally . . .?

I turned and found Mr. Still seated at a table, a thick rope of people already snaking around the room. I would have to wait at the back of the line. Discouraged, I looked for the end; instead people parted and I found myself kneeling at Mr. Still's side.

"Can you sign my book for me?" I asked.

"Sure," he said, eyes suddenly no longer hazel and blue, but shiny marbles of coal black, beams boring through me.... I was lost in the spotlight of Mr. Still's eyes.

"What do you want me to write?" Mr. Still said, removing a pen from his shirt pocket. "Whatever you like," I replied, staring up into the inky blackness that shrouded his iris.

"What's your name?" Mr. Still's voice called me. Avoiding my real name was a decades-old policy. Back again I went...staring at myself in the bathroom mirror, age three. Huge green eyes had earned me a number of nicknames, all rhyming with my primary nickname. Tish. "You'll be pretty when you're forty," I told my reflection. "No one will know your real name 'til then." My real name meant only one thing to me: old Polish woman. Only nuns, lawyers, police and Mommom called me by that name. "You'll grow into your name when you're older," I told the child in the glass.

Even my nametag at Hindman said Tish. I should have had some inkling that change was afoot when I found it under the wheels of a car in the upper parking lot and then, twice, inadvertently, on someone else. I just gave up wearing it. A huge triangle of emotion burst free of my throat, carving its way out the front of my neck. "Irene," I answered.

"Well, I haven't heard that name in years and years. It's a beautiful name, Irene." He put his pen to paper and I watched the slow tracing stillness of his hand, fighting back tears. I looked up at him. How could I tell him what he had just done? "You have made a great deal possible for me," I said. He blinked and color began to seep back into his eyes.

IRENE (TISH) MOSVOLD
Louisville, KY

WOLFPEN

To Dream Awhile

I took the path to Wolfpen Cabin.
Fall leaves crunched under my feet.
Birds sang above my head.
Weeping willows swayed proudly in the wind.
The coyote called out in the distance.
Squirrels scampered up the old oak tree.
A lizard slithered through the fence.
James Still with welcoming arms
On Wolfpen porch.
To dream for awhile.

BETTY BARGER PACE
Winchester, KY

A Day with James Still

For the last twelve years or so, I have been on a photographic journey in the Appalachians of Kentucky. In the words of James Still ("White Highways"):

I have gone out to the roads that go up and down
In smooth white lines, stoneless and hard. . .

I focused on people of rural towns, villages and hamlets to which Wal-Mart and McDonalds had not yet arrived. In this way, I probably short-changed the region in areas of obvious progress. And since I have not traveled rutted trails up the hollers, my photos did not show the extreme poverty that appeared in Shelby Lee Adams' photographic book, *Appalachian Portraits*. Concerned that I was not getting a complete picture of rural eastern Kentucky, I wanted to ask James Still to look over my collection and give me his opinion.

I had met Mr. Still once before, at a stuffy board meeting of the Appalachian Scholars Program at the University of Kentucky. I approached him apprehensively, but Mr. Still was enthusiastic. He invited me to the Hindman Settlement School for lunch. In December 1994, I made my first visit to the school. I left Lexington much too early, so on the way I stopped at a general store in Dwarf to take a photo of two elderly men. One of them said he learned his literature from Mr. Still back in the thirties.

When I finally found the school, we sat down at one of the tables in the large, empty dining hall. Jim, that's what he told me to call him, ate lunch there often. And when people were there, he liked to talk. Long after his second sandwich, he was telling me about Alabama, Texas, and his three diplomas that earned Mr. Still (sorry, I wasn't ready to call our master writer Jim yet) his early unpaid years at the Settlement School. He tried to recall the old gent from Dwarf, couldn't. A lot of young students had passed his way over the past sixty years.

"My pickup is right outside. Want to see my cabin?"
In his *Wolfpen Notebooks*, James Still wrote: "On a day in June 1939, I moved to an old log house between Dead Mare Branch and Wolfpen Creek, facing Little Carr Creek. To reach it from the county seat (that's Hindman) you traveled eight miles over a rutted wagon road, and then

James Still
in his early days
as librarian for the
Settlement School.
An early version of the
lending library, he carried
books to readers in places
not easily found by road.
(See Jim Hinsdale poem, p.71)

A later photograph of
James Still in one of his
characteristic straw hats.
*(Photograph by
Joyce Hancock)*

Cratis Williams, the pioneering scholar of Appalachian Studies,
washing dishes at the 1979 workshop.
(Photograph by Joyce Hancock)

Mike Mullins, Director of Hindman Settlement School
and the Workshop.
(Photograph by Judy Hensley)

Shirley Williams and Albert Stewart on the historic wall.
(Photograph by Joyce Hancock)

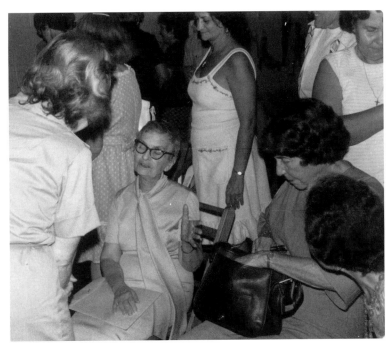

Harriette Arnow with students.

Barbara Smith
(Photograph by Joyce Hancock)

Jim Wayne Miller in conference with Debbie Spears.

Jack Higgs and Jeff Daniel Marion
(Photograph by Sam Linkous)

Silas House and Lee Smith walking Lee's illegal dog, Gracie.

Kitchen volunteers Lou Martin and Jan Walters Cook
surrounding Marie Bradby.
(Photograph by Ann Olson)

Dana Wildsmith in conversation during porch time.
(Photograph by Joyce Hancock)

Betty Smith
*(Photograph by
Judy Hensley)*

Sharyn McCrumb

Rita Quillen and Michael McFee
(Photograph by Joyce Hancock)

Betty Smith, Lee Smith, Mary Hodges, Hal Crowther
and others at the late night singing.
(Photograph by Alan McKellar, collage by Rene Hales)

Robert Morgan
(Photograph by Joyce Hancock)

Barbara Smith and Leatha Kendrick with
Mrs. Earp walking in the background.
(Photograph by Joyce Hancock)

Lee Smith, George Ella Lyon, and Angie DeBord.

Gurney Norman

Jonathan Greene, poet, publisher of Gnomon Press.
(Photograph by Joyce Hancock)

George Brosi, teacher, Appalachian scholar, bookseller.
(Photograph by Judy Hensley)

Paul Brett Johnson
(Photograph by Judy Hensley)

Chris Holbrook
(Photograph by Joyce Hancock)

Cheryl Ware
*(Photograph by
Judy Hensley)*

Jim Hinsdale during the first Jim Wayne Miller Memorial Lecture.
(Photograph by Joyce Hancock)

more than a mile up a creek bed." On this day in December, we traveled a paved highway with a wide white stripe, before turning off to the seclusion of his cabin at Wolfpen. Cold that day, Jim lit his gas heater and sat down in a rocker, next to a table stacked with books and journals. Pointed to a chair for me. "This area was peaceful before people moved in and started building." From assorted magazines, he picked up copies of the *Yale Review,* and the *Atlantic,* read some of his poems. He loved the mountains, had visited several in exotic places to help him appreciate his own "prisoning hills." When I said that I had done some climbing in the Pacific Cascades, he perked up. Wanted to know what it was like.

The shadows grew long. I had brought along my backpack, full of camera equipment, but felt too much awe to ask. He leaned forward. "You want to take some pictures?"

I did. Took several inside. Nervous and fumbling with my lighting, I ruined several shots with my mechanical Wista 4x5. He sat patiently, reading his *Yale Review,* best profile showing. "My favorite journal. you ought to read it."

I asked if I could take one photograph outside his doorway, where the washpan hung. There was a cold in the December air. As I photographed, he swept his hands around the yard, pointing to where the tulips, crocuses, daffodils, especially the daffodils, would bloom when I came back in April.

ALAN MACKELLAR
Lexington, KY

———————

In Kentucky

We went to look for a poet's soul
In a house devoid of his old man scent.
Bed and gourd and chimney rock
Spoke quaint and flat,
Rock-wailed well a Kodak shot,
Neat stacked jars and bowls
Yard-sale trash.

But by the rut-road out
The tall Joe-Pye weed insisted
On glory beyond its naming.
Lavender florets arched in dome
Swinging with butterfly wings, yellow-black,
A few blue-blacks clinging on the underside
In living fringe.
Butterflies danced
Round nodding domes of Joe Pye blooms.
Iridescent gold wings, blue Wings, veined with black
Moved in undulant pulse,
Singing his poems
In the quietude.

JOYCE COMPTON BROWN
Boiling Springs, NC

———————

James Still and Daniel

James Still drives [me, my best friend and her son, Daniel] up past Brinkley and Littcarr. A heron swoops down below us to Carr Creek. He tells us we are above the watershed. Troublesome, Wolfpen and Deadmare had been words. Now they are places of water and trees — of a man and a boy.

We reach the log house — not a log cabin. James Still is emphatic about that. An orange and white cat greets us and winds around his master's legs. Others have driven to his house. James Still is impatient to visit with Daniel, but he is hospitable, offering the adults some of his homemade brandy in the kitchen before taking us to his almost monastic room: bed, chair, table, typewriter, and books. He regales us with a story of Texas: a lonely story of a boy and woman on a remote cattle ranch. The typewritten words are locked in a briefcase that he raises to his lap and thumps. A story James Still says that he leaves for others to publish.

Three-year-old Daniel plays in lots of mowed running space and in plenty of shrub nooks for forts and castles. Before James Still drives us back to Hindman he and Daniel sit on the doorstep. I take a photograph.... You can almost see a cord linking them.

LINDA CALDWELL
Paint Lick, KY

James Still Leaves Wolfpen

Trembling, I listened: the summer sun
Had the chill of snow;
For I knew she was telling the bees of one
Gone on the journey we all must go.

—*John Greenleaf Whittier*

Did anyone think
to tell the bees? Beltane dawned
and they were busy at fencerows
hung with blackberry lace
and honeysuckle twining sweet.

Did anyone think
to drape the hive? Hang an inky
crepe upon the skep? Beltane bloomed,
were May baskets, the bright morning
custom, confused with memorials?

Did anyone think
to tell the bees? They surely were
the playfellows of his youth...who
danced Maypoles on Beltane morn,
clothed in garments of ballads.

Did anyone think
to lift the hive? Heave both boxes
the instant he was carried
from house to hollowed hillside
to reside eternal guardian of Troublesome?

JANE HICKS
Blountville, TN

from Hindman Homegoing

I had met James Still before, but at Hindman he was fully in his element and much activity buzzed around him as he royally held forth at lunchtime and dinnertime. Although he and my husband, poet Jeff Daniel Marion, were longtime friends and spoke easily together, I was primarily a listener, an appreciative audience for his tales. The last time I saw Mr. Still, two years before his death, he told us he had bought English violets to be planted on his grave. It gave me chills, but endeared him to me in a way I had never felt. He seemed to see me for the first time, to be telling me his plans, as if he understood I also loved violets and he knew they were the flower of my birth month, February. Writing this so near spring, I wonder if they are blooming now on the still-fresh mound overlooking the entrance of the dining hall, where on that fine May day the guard sounded the news of his passing.

LINDA PARSONS MARION
Knoxville, TN

———————

I first attended The Hindman Settlement School Writers Conference in 1992 and was enthralled by the atmosphere of the place, inspired by the excellence of the teaching staff and amazed at the variety of talent among the attendees. My writing began to improve almost immediately and I got to thinking that this was occurring because of some creative form of osmosis.

One night in the dining room, carrying my dinner plate to a table, I stumbled and brushed the arm of that wonderful man of words, James Still. Mr. Still looked up at me, grinned and said, "Careful! You might just catch something," to which I replied: "I certainly hope so."

VIRGINIA DULWORTH
Lexington, KY

V

CLASS NOTES

First Lesson

Morning, crossing Troublesome,
      hung artistry arrests,
            an overnight creation spun
          cable to railing to brace.

Filaments from body drawn
      converge to thready eye.
            Straight stitches circle out full round
          in rings and rings and rings.

Mist beads, sized and spaced just so,
      sag strands to gravity.
            Slant sunrays glimmer, glisten through,
          parsed colors prismed out.

Whisper breeze sheer netting billows,
      dew jewels quiver, shimmer, wink,
            while hunkered in some crevice deep,
          deft weaver watches, waits.

Winged tree seed, loosed and craving earth,
      spins down, drifts down, copters in —
            snagged now, snared, collaged midair
          with ant wing, nest down, catkin, gnat.

JIM TOMLINSON
Berea, KY

Dear Sara,

I have had a good week here at the Writer's Workshop even if it did rain three days straight. Troublesome Creek was swollen to the top of its banks. My shoes were making juicy, squishy, sounds by the time I walked to the James Still Learning Center. It did not dampen my spirits a bit, though.

We go to two classes and then its time for lunch. Mike Mullins does not aim for us to go hungry. We have writing for children after that and then listen to participants reading their writing for an hour. Its time for a huge supper. There is little rest — usually we are writing assignments. The big dinner bell rings. It's time to hear the instructor readings. Next, mountain musicians entertain us with rolicky Bluegrass and gospel music. Toes a-tapping, hands a-clapping, we keep time as banjos and guitars and bass violins hold us enthralled. Afterwards, we go to a music party in a cabin where dulcimers, and banjos are played and ballads are sung till everyone is exhausted. Finally we turn in for a few winks.

We walked in early morning and saw two brown ducks in tandem swimming the waters of Troublesome Creek. Everything gives us joy. Laughter comes easy in this place.

RUTH ANN ANTLE
Russell Springs, KY

Observations of a Commuter Student

August 1988

I drive from Prestonsburg to Hindman on the new Route 80, hills sliced open for pavement, an easy thirty-mile trip impossible when I left eastern Kentucky in the early 70s.

Crowded into the children's room of the Knott County Public Library, about a dozen of us strain to hear Richard Hague and Robert Morgan above the metallic hum of the window air conditioner. Our clothes stick to us, the paper we've typed our poems on sticks to our fingers. I think this whole place is sticking to me. Jim Wayne Miller gives me a six-inch stack of articles about Appalachian literature so I can teach it at Virginia Tech.

August 1991

This year George Ella Lyon is teaching playwriting in the basement of the Knott County Public Library. At one point in an exercise, she cuts paper for us with Swiss army knife scissors, a gift from her husband. She says our words are gifts to readers. I know her poems and books are gifts. Denise Giardina is here, so serious and quiet and shy but strong in her beliefs, like her character Carrie in *Storming Heaven*.

I hear Lee Smith's laugh in the dining hall before I see her. I knew I'd recognize her from the photos on her book jackets but I hadn't thought of her voice. Her laugh is rich and high and full, like a musical instrument, sort of a cross between a flute and a mandolin, full of down-to-earth delight. Now I have that laugh in my head just as I have her characters and stories in my head.

Cassie Mullins baby-sits my five-month-old daughter in the Settlement School office while I attend classes. I spend my lunch hour on the floor feeding and playing with baby Lauren, then rush back to class and scribble furiously. James Still says if you can write poetry, you can write fiction, and I begin to believe him.

1993

In his class on Appalachian Literature, Jim Wayne Miller reads Pinckney Benedict's "The Sutton Pie Safe"— the entire story — with great enjoyment, relishing each word, each image, each interaction between characters, the clash of the old and the new in Southern Appalachia. He reads it as if he were offering us something mysterious and delicious and important.

KATHY MAY
Charlottesville, VA

_____

In one of my early poetry workshops in the Community Building room overlooking the old swimming pool, one of Rita Quillen's assignments was to write a poem in the voice of a rock. I wasn't able to do it. But that assignment has always been in the back of my mind, and this past summer, more than 10 years later, I produced a few words in that stoic persona that satisfy me. Thanks, Rita.

CHARLIE HUGHES
Nicholasville, KY

Remembering Appalachian Writers Workshops

Wilma Dykeman sent me to the Appalachian Writers Workshop [in] 1980.... In the early years, classes were held in the Knott County Public Library on campus. Crossing the wooden bridge over Troublesome Creek in early morning fog was enchanting. Along that path, I recall Herb E. Smith of Appalshop walking backward, while filming Harriette Arnow for a documentary.

George Ella Lyon's lecturing was superb. One morning, in the library basement, we students crowded closely to catch George Ella's every word, while a fly persistently buzzed her face. George Ella patiently brushed it away and continued her talk. The fly suddenly disappeared and George Ella gulped. "Did you swallow it?" a rogue called from the back row.

George Ella managed a surprised smile and said, "I think so." She then calmly continued her remarks.

Midweek in the 1987 workshop, Maggie Anderson offered to critique extra poetry, and I gave her a few poems. At my conference, she asked, "Do you ever write about your own family?"

So unexpected was this that my tears welled. "I can't handle that," I explained. Maggie gently insisted I try; and this huge barrier was broken with "Morning-glories" that later won a writing award and was published. I'll always be grateful that Maggie's faith spurred me to write and publish most of my "thread poems" series.....

Jim Wayne Miller's tremendous influence benefited workshop students, both through teaching and mailed notes and advice. Through Jim Wayne's contact, Seven Buffaloes Press published my Pearl poems in book form and in anthologies for several years.

PATRICIA SHIRLEY
Knoxville, TN

At a summer workshop at Hindman Settlement School in the 1970s, I was in a class taught by the author Harriette Arnow. We wrote short stories, and "Footprints In The Hollow" was my short story. My teacher urged me to write a novel and my short story became the first chapter in my book *Heritage of the Hills*.

ELIZABETH HILL
Procious, WV

A Kentucky Literature Teacher Meets Hindman

In the late 1980's as English chair of Gallatin County High School, I became frustrated with having to teach English Literature to my senior kids who had no intention after graduation of ever darkening the doors of an institution of learning.

In the summer of 1988, cleaning out our English department bookroom shortly after I became chair, I happened across 28 copies of a small anthology, Joy Pennington's *Selected Kentucky Literature*, 28 copies of James Still's *River of Earth*, and 28 copies of Jesse Stuart's *The Thread that Runs So True*. Hardly used, the books had collected dust since the phase elective fad of the seventies had phased out.

Eureka! I incorporated Stuart's novel, some stories and poems from Pennington's anthology, and the Still novel into my "average" class. In the unsigned evaluation essays I collected after the course was complete and the kids knew their grades, the sections of Kentucky lit were the favorite sections: most said *River of Earth* was the best book ever, and all suggested changing the course to strictly Kentucky lit....

In the fall of 1990, my father died, and I took on the responsibility of running his small farm as well as my own. Mom sold off the cattle, and I baled the pastures four times that summer to keep them clean. Sometime just before the deadline for the writers workshop, Mom read about it in the Cincinnati paper. "You need a break," she said. She knew I had taken to writing stories for my students. "Why don't I send you to this writers thing?"

Imagine! Gurney Norman, author of *Kinfolks* and *Divine Right's Trip* was teaching short story. When I gave the commencement address to my students in '90, I had included a small parody of Divine Right's scene in the bus station. George Ella Lyon, whose play, *Braids,* had so moved me when I saw it performed at one of the Berea seminars, whose essays and poems I had used, was teaching children's stories. Poet Jim Wayne Miller was teaching the history of Appalachian literature. I had encountered Miller's work for the first time in a Mellon seminar. Denise Giardina was teaching novel. I read from *Storming Heaven* to my classes. They loved Giardina's baseball game between the union and non-union miners. When one of my AP kids had trouble finding enough research for her paper on Giardina, she'd written the author. Denise had answered her letter and sent copies of articles and newspaper clippings.

James Still was on campus as well as Albert Stewart. When I first sent out a few poems, I had sent them to Mr. Stewart. While he'd given up editorship of *Appalachian Heritage* some time earlier, he returned the poems and wrote a nice letter of encouragements and given me the address of Sidney Farr. What more could an English teacher ask for than to learn from such folks?

Hindman was much more than I could ever have hoped for. The people whom I had hoped to learn from accepted me as an equal. Not only did I get to listen to them, I ate at their tables and became friends with most. Barbara Smith, one of the two instructors at that workshop with who I was unfamiliar, taught non-fiction. Like an idiot, instead of twenty pages I sent her a complete manuscript. She read the whole thing and liked it. When she'd finished reading her non-fiction manuscripts and completed her conferences, she sought me out and offered to look at my poetry, something she certainly didn't have to do. From that afternoon with Barbara Smith, I learned how to edit. In addition, she took one poem for *Grab-a-Nickel*. It was the first thing I had published since college....

I attended several consecutive Hindman workshops after that first one, and all were equally rewarding.... For at least one week a year, Hindman in Knott County, Kentucky, is a magical place. I intend to return again.

JIM HINSDALE
Tryon, NC

———

In later years Lee Smith arrived with her husband Hal Crowther and dog Gracie in tow. Lee's laugh could locate her within a mile radius piercing many heavy duty deep serious conversations about writing. And I bonded with Hal, another Yankee like myself, married to a Southern belle of mysterious manners and lore. I remember one night Hal and I were corralled by John Egerton who still had stories to tell and in the wee hours did not want to let us fade into the night.

Many alumnae of the workshops would later emerge with books (Silas House, Leatha Kendrick, Dana Wildsmith, and others) and some lucky few would even be anointed by Mike to come back to help lead workshops. The heritage of the workshop is a rich one in writings and friendships through the long years of its existence.

JONATHAN GREENE
Franklin County, KY

from Tracing Trips to Hindman

In recent years, I've gone to Hindman specifically to attend the non-fiction writing classes of Joyce Dyer and Hal Crowther. I admired her work as the editor of *Bloodroot* and the author of *In a Tangled Wood,* and I admired his columns in *The Oxford American* and his book *Cathedrals of Kudzu,* the title of which was apparently inspired by Hindman landscapes. And, of course, I wanted to be in the presence of Jack Higgs and to attend his Appalachian Literature classes. Who else can dazzle you by connecting Greek concepts of humor and beauty to Sut Lovingood and James Still and then make you laugh so hard that you can't take good notes!

....I like the peace and quiet of the place. It's the only time during the year when I spend a whole week without television, when the only sounds I notice are birds, the dinner bell, and human voices. The energy I carry home from that stillness and those voices sustains me.

SANDRA L. BALLARD
Boone, NC

The Divine Trickster Lectures
at the Writing Conference
(Hindman, August 2000)
for Jack Higgs

That great bear of a man
hitching up his breeches,
laughing at himself:
The divine trickster, come to call

Illumining souls
beyond their capacity to hold,
he draws his golden circle
to include the least of those gathered here.

His hand, larger than life,
holds a book which he passes
to each in turn,
the tip of his finger
almost brushing theirs. †

Dr. Higgs would be modest about his influence and would, in fact, discourage praise from others. Like his hero, Sut Lovingood, he would pronounce a disclaimer to knowing anything of any consequence. Nevertheless, his affirmation of each person's efforts has been a tremendous encouragement to Appalachian writers for many years.

While listening to one of his lectures at Hindman in which he projected the painting of God reaching down to Adam, their fingertips almost touching, on the overhead screen, I could not help but see the analogy.

EVELYN McAMIS BALES
Kingsport, TN

Danny Marion's Ass is Upstairs,
or Hindman Hind-Sight

"Danny Marion's Class Is Upstairs"— Elaine leans back against the sign that directs us to Jeff Daniel Marion's poetry class on the second floor of the James Still building. Rebecca notices how nicely Elaine blocks the first two letters of "Class" in the sign behind her head. Crowing irreverently that we had better get our asses upstairs, too, Rebecca urges us to join the rush to find seats. But, of course, I am the one who pauses to write down "Danny Marion's Ass Is Upstairs" in my journal, and I miss the beginning of class again.

This must be the same day that Elaine and Rebecca first meet over the cosmos planted in James Still's garden outside the dormitory and strike up an unusually fast friendship. Oh, it's the cosmos, I tell them. It is my conviction that cosmos has a strange effect on people. When I comment how their dished petals operate like satellites positioned to pick up information from the larger cosmos, you know, the immortals, to transfer it to us nearby receivers, mere mortal writerly types, Elaine and Rebecca allow as how I might be onto something, um, cosmic.

Where else can you explore things like this out loud but at Hindman's workshop for writers, I wonder. William Churchill's advice is that "audacity is the ticket." Those are also the parting words of James Still at the close of his conversation with us that day — August 1, 1995.

James Still died this year in his 95th year. Even now I struggle to hear the cosmos. I forgot to ask: if audacity is the ticket, where are we going? Oh, never mind; just save me a seat.

BARB CHILDERS
Kingsport, TN

A Writing Class

I remember walking downhill from the Stone building, crossing the bridge over the creek, the morning air still cool and damp, birds flickering around a Rose of Sharon tree in bloom, sunlight in the dewy grass of the playing field. I joined people going up to the library, into a class to be taught by Chris Holbrook and Gurney Norman.

Chris handed out copies of only the first pages of short stories by Chekhov, Maugham, and others, and in his quiet, purposeful way, suggested exactly how it was that some of these openings did intrigue us more than others. He showed where sentences written one way instead of another made you want to keep reading; explained how feelings you'd had but not understood on reading had been evoked.

Then Gurney came into the room, jaunty, peremptory, serious: "All right, let's get started, folks!" He didn't wait for us to appear ready. "Take up that notebook and start writing right now, right here, what is going on in your life that is urgent, pressing, has you worried or excited. It's hell out there, people, there's hardly even the time to be doing something like this. Let's get with it."

To illustrate he told of having just decided, for reasons you could tell he'd long considered, to go disinter certain ancestors and move the remains to another site. The reasons he gave I don't recall exactly — having to do, I think, with where was the true homeplace — but I remember they were persuasive. Yet he seemed unnerved by his own determination. "Think about that." He looked up at us. "I'm about to go dig these people *up*."

It was strange, real, and it shook us up. A need to do right; a need to make peace. What is essential? Time is precious. Read as a writer. See as one. Get your sentences right.

Now, eleven years later, still loving the work of writing daily, I appreciate more than ever that example, the message to write with discrimination, to waste no time, to write what matters. I believe we all got started that very hour.

DAVID TODD
Silver Spring, MD

————

I have a distinct workshop memory from Hindman that has stayed with me and helped me define what a writing community is to me. I was struggling through the M.F.A. program at Penn State when I had a workshop at Hindman with Kay Byer. She instructed us to write something that we remembered vividly as children. My mind had been cluttered with a thousand different things when I very suddenly started writing about the fear of God that I had as a child when I would see the swooning and shouting of people around me in church. I had written about revivals before, but never on the level of how it appeared to me as a child. I was shocked by the detail that came to the poem almost immediately; the flesh of old women in front of me that jiggled around as they raised their arms and their shirts shook loose from their skirts, the sound of feet behind me in the very beginning shufflings of someone getting in the spirit. I couldn't believe the speed with which this poem left me. By the end of the week, I had polished it and read it at the microphone on one of the last nights at Hindman.

The best part about that workshop poem was that it came in such detail and with such little provocation and that the experience of polishing it during the week made it feel like a community effort. I had never, even in M.F.A. workshops, felt that degree of support for a poem, that degree of investment from my peers. Jane Hicks, Pia Seagrave and especially Kay Byer helped me pare down the language and really focus on that child's point of view. By the time I gave the reading of the poem, it felt like something that had been lifted into the light (which was appropriate enough for the subject matter). It proved to me the ease with which ideas and creations can be provoked and honed in on when the community of people working with you is "on the same page."

I went back to Penn State after that workshop demanding more of those peers, those instructors, and that M.F.A. program itself. It was a rather pinnacle moment for me because I realized that no degree or program was bigger or better than the people who form that community of writers. And it brought home with total clarity the fact that Appalachian writers, and specifically Hindman writers, are my community. And I think because of that realization, I did not feel that textbook desperation or feeling of being cut off when I graduated the M.F.A. program and was cut loose on my own. It seemed very obvious to me that the M.F.A. degree looks good on paper, but the real training and preparation I got during those years came during the summer vacations when I was back in the hills of Kentucky with my people.

LISA PARKER
New York City, NY

---

from A Teacher

My first Appalachian Writers Workshop was in 1986. I was so impressed with Ellesa Clay High who taught a descriptive writing class. The assignment was to compose a paragraph describing something in the room. Suggested topics were a window or chair; one classmate described her big toe. The most animated subject was our teacher, Ellesa Clay High, and I wrote the following about her:

"Her hair is thick as Pocahawnes' and pulled to one side over the right shoulder. The quick eyes pull a response from even the most stubborn listener. A nose as thin as a plow stock riding a high ridge takes one down the steep slope from the felt brim of her hat."

In a second paragraph she asked us to explain why we chose this topic:

"She reminds me of a good friend, the dark hair and brushing it back with the backs of her fingers. I wonder what might happen if they met. Would they think they look alike, immediately become friends, or repel like two south poles? I have always heard we have an identical twin in the world."

When she read this out loud, she interlocked her fingers and pulled, to demonstrate a connection. She was moved by the art which she had inspired.

ARTIE ANN BATES
Blackey, KY

Ghost Writer

"Mom, How do you keep getting me in these messes? I told you I had changed my mind and did not want to attend this workshop. Now I have to walk down this hillside and talk to a published author about a story I supposedly wrote, that I have never even seen before."

In the spring of 1996 I expressed interest to my mother about attending the Appalachian Writers Workshop at Hindman Settlement School that summer. After mentioning it to Mom I didn't think much more about it. Mom told me that you had to write something and send it in to be reviewed before being accepted to the workshop. I said o.k. A few more weeks passed and Mom reminded me about having to write something. I told her that I thought I had changed my mind about attending. She said, "Oh, come on, Melissa, write something so that I can mail it, or I will write something for you." I replied, "Oh, please don't. I will try to get something to you."

I really did put it to the back of my mind until Mom told me I had been accepted. "But I didn't write anything." Mom explained that she had written something for me and mailed it in for review.

"What did you write?" I asked.

"A story." Mom replied.

"What is the story about?" I asked getting more nervous by the minute.

"Old shoes."

"Old shoes! What about them?" I couldn't have heard her correctly.

"Oh, don't worry, Melissa, you can read over the story before you talk to one of the authors about it."

"I have to talk to one of the resident authors about a story that I wrote, when I really didn't write the story?"

"Yes."

"Can't I just write something and take it with me and tell them the truth?"

"No! You can write something but don't tell them the truth."

So here I was at the Hindman Settlement School getting ready to walk down to the dining hall to talk to Barbara Smith about a story that I supposedly wrote, but I had never even seen because my mom forgot to bring a copy, so I could read the story before this meeting.

As I got to the dining hall, the news camera appeared to tape some of the workshop for the local news. Lo and behold, if they didn't come into the dining hall and tape some of my meeting with Barbara Smith.

She would ask me questions about why I wrote this or that. I would have to ask her if I could please take a moment to reread that section, that it had been a while since I had written this piece. I would quickly read what my mother had written for me, then answer Ms. Smith's question, while the TV camera was filming us. Barbara had to have known that something was wrong, but I never let on. I just smiled and did the best I could. I might not be a very good writer, but I would say I played my part well that day.

MELISSA LILES
Greenup, KY

A Cinquain, Remembering Robert Morgan
(Appalachian Writers Workshop, 1990)

Steady,
accented voice,
a smiling mentoring —
the tones we need, advice we crave —
just right.

JUDY KLARE
The Plains, OH

Someone in the poetry class workshop said, "Oh, there's Robert Morgan." He sat down beside me. All I knew was that he had a best-selling book thanks to Oprah picking it up for her book club and that he was to speak here at Hindman. I had sent in a handful of poems on a whim for my first year at the workshop and I had no idea who the man sitting next to me was.

"So, how's Oprah?" I began our conversation.

"Oh, she's fine. I didn't get to spend too much time with her. She's all business when the cameras stop rolling. But her staff was certainly accommodating," he allowed.

I asked about the particulars for the book discussion that was aired on television. Did they go to a restaurant? "No," he said politely and told me about the mock library setup where the discussion was held. Robert Morgan told me Oprah offered wine but he refused so as to keep "his wits about him."

I had met high school English and community college teachers up to this point and I knew Oprah often chose novice writers.

I continued my attempts to make small talk with Robert Morgan.

"So.....do you teach anywhere?" I intoned.

"I am getting ready to retire from Cornell," he said.

I thought, "Oh, shit...that's not a community college!"

He was so gracious and it was only later, after I had read my little poem (sharing my copy with this distinguished author) that I found out Robert Morgan was nationally known as a poet before he was known as a novelist. When the critiquing began, I handed my copy of the poem to him.

"Be kind," I looked at him and said.

He was.

DEBORAH COOPER
Cynthiana, KY

———————

Gleanings from Hindman

ON JOB ADVICE FOR ASPIRING WRITERS

"Work evenings as a waitress in a good place with short hours — but make sure there are plenty of bus boys so you don't have to do the heavy work."
— Harriette Arnow

ON SCHOLARLY WRITING

"They can organize material — but it's largely indigestible."
— James Still

ON RESEARCH TECHNIQUES

"I find inspiration from lines overheard while hanging out in malls. I insist on calling it research, but it's very hard to justify to the people you live with."
— Lee Smith

ON THE NEED FOR REVISION

"When you paint a room, the first coat looks awful,
but the second coat does wonders."
— George Ella Lyon

ON WRITING SHORT FICTION

"The best place to start a short story is as near the end as possible."
— James Still

ON THE APPALACHIAN WRITERS WORKSHOP

"This week is more than writing —
it's the breathing in and out of ideas."
— Gurney Norman

PATRICIA L. HUDSON
Knoxville, TN

Some of the most important memories I have of the Workshop are those of affirmation from instructors: Gurney Norman telling me in a very gentle, careful voice, as I sat weeping, that he liked my short story; Dr. Jack Higgs surprising me by discussing the literature of my region as deserving of serious study and approbation; Lee Smith greeting me by name and asking, with contagious good spirits, "Will you let me read your story?"

And from individuals who, whatever their place in the hierarchy, for a moment opened themselves so fully that I recognized in them the same heady love I have for writing: Ron Rash saying without a blink of self-conscious embarrassment that he had not been able to sleep the night before, for thinking about the sounds of certain words together; Jack Higgs standing beside the person whom he had asked to read from James Still's *River of Earth,* his head tilted, his hand moving like an orchestra conductor's to the rich music of Still's language; Sandra Aldrich, interrupting my practice reading to say, "Wait a minute, wait a minute. That was good. Read that part again."

Support and encouragement, a sense of community, and an ease to the loneliness in which many of us live our artistic lives. That's it. That's some it, anyway.

DEBORAH TILSON CLARK
Troutdale, VA

VI

DINING HALL & DISHES

From My Diary at Hindman
(August, 1989)

I love the down-home breakfasts we're getting here… bacon and eggs, bran muffins one day and pancakes, syrup and sausage the next. One morning we had biscuits with sausage gravy. Heavenly. I've seen it being served in some restaurants, but have always turned up my nutrition-conscious nose. No way to watch the cholesterol this week. I'm into decadent eating and lapping it up.

ARLINE MCCARTHY
Athens, OH

———————

One of the special features [of the Workshop]…was mealtime in the May Stone Building. These were always filled with jokes, laughter, and sharing recipes. At least once during the week we had to take a turn in the kitchen, cleaning up and doing dishes. Jim Wayne even took a turn with a dishrag cleaning tables. One of the songs we sang was an old timer, "She'll be Coming 'Round the Mountain."

During the week authors Verna Mae Slone and Joy Bale Boone came by to visit. I bought Mrs. Slone's book, *What My Heart Wants to Tell* [and] took a picture of Verna Mae, Joy, and James Still sitting on the stone wall outside the dining hall.

BETTY J. SPARKS
Flatwoods, KY

A Hindman Recipe

Let the swelter sweat of August
steam the ridgepockets on Troublesome:
make way Pigeon Roost and Rowdy for the word
workers toting yellow pencils to stir
what lies in these satchels of memory,
hankering for the yeast of stories
to rise: here the miller's finest flour
still sifts into waiting hands:
there will be swarp and song, feast
aplenty, a brew to set porches rocking:
there are no limits here; always fresh
bread to sop this word stew, art.

In my satchel of memory Hindman snapshots abound: James Still ambling across the dining hall, silverware tucked in his back pocket, plate piled high, snatches of talk from our porch visits ("How do you like your new car, Mr. Still?" "Well, we keep going together, but we're not married yet."); Al Stewart grinning, brushing back his mop of fine hair, telling me how much he admires my straw hat, identical to his; Harriette Arnow looking dagger straight at her husband who has taken a seat by the ladder into the loft of James Still's log house: "Now, Harold, I know what you're doing — trying to look up women's dresses when they climb to see the loft;" laughter and song spilling down the hillside late into the night, sounds of voices adrift on the air; Jim Wayne Miller's typewriter clacking steadily at 3 a.m. — Jim himself at 7:30 a.m., leaning on the wall outside the dining hall, coffee cup in one hand, cigarette in the other, his white shirt gleaming in morning mist, his dark hair slicked back.

These snapshots I hold close because I know when I return yearly to Hindman I will not see them, but their spirits will be there, mingling among this homecoming of word gatherers, listening and reveling in the celebration.

JEFF DANIEL MARION
Knoxville, TN

———

Suppertime at Hindman

1. Jack Asks a Question

At dinner the first night, I sat down
With Jack Higgs and a half dozen strangers.
Jack beamed at us all and began to ask
Each one, "Where're *you* from?" As if
Knowing our places was simply the first
Step in knowing, well, anything worth
Knowing. Every writer understands that,
Right? Not necessarily. I remember a poet
Living outside Black Mountain
Who'd not let her toddler be tended
By mountain women. *I don't want him learning*
To talk as if he came from here, she explained,
All the while looking round at the mountains
Beginning to sull up at sunset. Like me,
Wishing I could unleash a freak blizzard

Dining Hall & Dishes 111

Or skull-bashing hailstorm. Perhaps you are
Wondering where this woman came from,
But I didn't ask. Didn't dare to.
She might have glared back at me,
Such emptiness glazing her eyes
As to render me mute. Nowhere,
I imagine her answering. Nowhere,
Nowhere. And what then
Would Jack Higgs have said to that?

2. Jack Welcomes the Poet from Nowhere to Hindman

You might as well sit down at my table.
The food's good here. The people are
Friendly. The music's like nothing else
You ever heard. You can listen to Troublesome Creek
Babble all night long, if you're not singing
Up on the hilltop with Betty and Lisa and
Jane and the rest of those hillbilly women.
Right now you can hear Lee speaking clear through
This dinnertime ruckus, and if you will let it,
Her voice takes you right along,
Sidewinding up Bethel Mountain or maybe
Down Hoot Owl Holler where old Granny
Younger's been waiting for someone
Like you, scared to open your mouth
For fear you'll sound like somebody
Who comes from somewhere, a real singing,
Storified, well-off-the-beaten track place.
Like a hick, you know.
Like me.

Like the whole blessed lot of us
Telling each other over white beans and cornbread
Where *we* come from: wherever the words
We love take root like catbrier and live.

KATHRYN STRIPLING BYER
Cullowhee, NC

Late to the Table

I am a sixty year old biology professor, and never likely to be a noted writer or biologist. If one objective of writing is to bring catharsis, understanding, and a sense of art to us as writers, then it doesn't matter whether my efforts are published or not. Hindman has more than fulfilled its mission for me. From the dining hall to the workshops, my plate has been filled.

The thought of writing, especially for publication, had never crossed my mind. Then, a few years ago I wrote a few anecdotal stories from my father's oral repertoire about the life of his family and neighbors in our Blue Ridge community of North Cove, North Carolina. My objective was simple, to keep my family heritage alive. My wife, Joyce, read a few of them and actually laughed out loud. I was shocked; she never laughs at my attempts at humor. She said that I should try to develop some of the stories, and she encouraged me to send something to Hindman. Reluctantly I did. The experience has not only been a communal feast, but has also given me the incentive to keep writing. Sydney Farr worked with me that first year, forcing me to give up many of my precious words; she later accepted a story of mine for publication in *Appalachian Heritage.*

The gifts of motivation, encouragement, excellence of modeling and a spiritual camaraderie are my Hindman experience. Hindman makes great writers real, especially when I am slopping around in the kitchen with them, washing dishes. Hindman is like a fine dessert that satisfies, that I look forward to, that has a nice chocolate icing of good old acoustic music each night. And by the way, Betty Smith is a candle on top, casting a warm light over those wonderful evenings.

LES BROWN
Boiling Springs, NC

Green Peppers and A Straw Hat

At Tuesday's lunch, Mr. James Still pulled out a ladderback chair and sat down by ME in the dining room. ME, eating at the same table with our guru! My gosh, what would I say? What could I say? Nearly dumbstruck, I managed a "hello." Mr. Still nodded in acknowledgment a "hello" as kitchen helpers placed food before him as if he were royalty. With our elbows nearly touching, we crumbled cornbread into our soup beans in silence.

On that hot humid sweltering dog day in August, Mr. Still brought forth a shiny green pepper, not a bell, but a long, funnel-shaped one. Fascinated, I watched as he lifted it from his shirt pocket and laid it on the oil-cloth table beside his plate. From the corners of my eyes, I stole glances as he cut off bits of his pepper and ate them between spoonfuls of soup beans.

I come from a large mountain family that yattered on and on while eating. Silence around the table denoted sickness or guilt or some such. Anyway, I felt pressured to say something because I could stand the silence no more. I asked my simple question, "Is that the hot kind?" Honestly, Mr. Still's expression had failed to register any changes when he took a bite. To add to the situation of no air conditioning, the overhead fans whirled above us, driving the heat of the nearby kitchen around us too. Yet no beads of perspiration arose on Mr. Still's forehead. More silence. Oh boy.

Finally a reply, "Yes, I eat one every day from my garden."

Hallelujah, I was saved.

His garden! There it was. The curtains parted. I had gardened most of my life and all of a sudden we were off, discussing vegetables, flowers, weeds and seeds. He told me he had turned to gardening as a solace when he returned from duty after WW II. He munched his pepper as if it bordered on sweetness. Someone brought him a piece of cake. He ate on. Gardening had seen him through those difficult times he told me. Gardening has seen me through tough ones as well....

When he returned home, he couldn't write or do anything. He was in an awful state. "I just sat in my doorway and did nothing for a year."

What I gleaned from all this was that notable writers were human beings just like myself. Knowing Mr. Still had not written for a year gave me reassurance and comfort because I too went for periods without writing. Sitting in my "doorway" like Mr. Still, I can always meditate. I know I will write when the right time presents itself.

I miss seeing Mr. Still come into the dining room holding his straw hat behind him. I miss his deep voice around the dining table at Hindman where I know for sure something happened to me. He and others gave me the courage to be a writer.

JAN WALTERS COOK
Lexington, KY

from Finding Home

My reason for attending [the Workshop] was Lee Smith's *Fair and Tender Ladies,* which made me bawl for an hour after I finished it. Graduate school had killed my love of books, where we dissected literature and concentrated mostly on secondary sources. Lee Smith and Ivy Rowe brought me back to life. I wanted to meet the person responsible for my rebirth. And I wasn't disappointed. Lee's class was fantastic, but it was even better washing supper dishes with her, elbow to elbow. Something about sticking your hands in soapy water erases boundaries, making instant friends.

Then she critiqued my stories. Yikes. I thought my head would explode with all the blood rushing to it. "These stories are so true and funny!" she said. I couldn't believe it. She even asked me to read "Cremation 101: The Paper Route Memoirs" to the class, and when I declined out of shyness, she said, "Is it all right if I read it?" The next morning, 60 people laughed as she read my story. Then I could feel 60 stomachs turning as she got to the embalming part. I started realizing the power of words.

Then two women came up to me. The first said, "I know you are the one who wrote the story because you were sitting there cringing while the rest of us were laughing, and I want you to know that you've changed my life. "I'm going to get cremated!"

The second person was George Ella Lyon, and she asked me if I'd ever thought of writing for young people, which was a question that changed my life. Since that day in 1994, I've published three middle-grade novels for children, for which I have Hindman to thank, and Barbara Smith for suggesting that I give it a try.

CHERYL WARE
Elkins, WV

Poets at Workshops

Like half-starved refugees,
they break from their cells,
emaciated ribs protruding
like tiny pipelines,
eyes, sunken scavengers
that prey for nourishment,
salivary glands dry, tongue splitting.

They eavesdrop in lines, at tables,
behind doors, capture half sentences,
scan the want ads of journals and newspapers,
send out messengers.
Fingers parch and ache in the August heat
from scribbling pages
and not a page a poem.
They lie at the doors of rooms
like beggars straining for a phrase, a line,
a word to fit into stanzas,
any morsel that would taste delicious in a poem.

SHIRLEY R. CHAFIN
Paintsville, KY

We spend much of every day projecting images that others expect from us. When we arrive at Hindman, we take off those masks and show our true selves — that inner being we keep hidden from people easily shocked by a writer's quirky mind.

The following glimpse embodies that spirit:

• The second year Kitty and I attended Hindman, we opted [for] lunch dishwashing duty mid-week. No one we knew was on our crew, so we started the normal get-to-know-you chitchat. One woman told us about her novel set in 16th Century France. Someone said; "It must have been interesting doing the research." She replied, "I didn't have to. I was there in my former life." And we all kept washing and listening to her experiences as if she was telling us about what had happened at breakfast.

KATHY J. COMBS
Houston, TX

Kudzu Jelly

One August morning while I climbed the hills at Hindman Settlement School, a woman from the Writers Workshop hurried towards me. She clutched a bouquet of orchid-colored flowers in both hands. *Kudzu,* she said. *It's blooming!*

I didn't know kudzu did that, I answered. *Where?*

She pointed to the top of the hill. I hiked up, entered the giant's bedroom, bravely peered into the abyss of one of his wide, green sleeves. There it was — a kudzu flower in full bloom! Why he hides these up his sleeves…I can't tell you.

RECIPE FOR KUDZU FLOWER JELLY

Yield: If you use 5 ounce jars, this recipe will yield about 6 jars of jelly.

INGREDIENTS

4 cups fresh kudzu blossoms, clean of stems and leaves, washed and well drained
1 Tablespoon lemon juice
$1\frac{3}{4}$ ounces pectin
5 cups granulated sugar

INSTRUCTIONS

Bring 4 cups water to rolling boil. Stir in kudzu flowers, cook 2 minutes. Remove from heat. Let stand for 12 hours, then strain liquid. Keep liquid, discard flowers. Pour liquid in kettle, add lemon juice and pectin, bring to rolling boil. Stir in sugar. Stir constantly until liquid reaches second rolling boil. Boil 2 to 3 minutes, remove from heat, skim off foam.

Pour into sterilized jars and seal with airtight lids. Place jars on rack and submerge in boiling water bath for 5 minutes. When cool enough to touch, tighten lids and turn upside down for 2 to 5 hours.

• Do not use flowers from kudzu that has been sprayed with herbicide.

• Make sure green stems or leaves are removed from flowers. These give jelly a bitter taste.

ELAINE CAVANAUGH
Hartland, WI

Hindman

The waters of Troublesome
Dry to a trickle in the July heat.
We rock on the porch, hike the hill,
Read to each other in the dorms at midnight
Working words into poems, stories,
Bridges across the spaces between us.

Like the countless stitches,
That pattern the quilts
Hanging in the Great Hall,
Our work weaves in among those whose words live on
In this place of writing and renewal —
Mr. Still, Jim Wayne, Albert, Harriette, Cratis....

Hungry, we wait in line at the Dining Hall
For dinners of soup beans and cornbread,
Taco salad, and talk. All of us —
Mike from High Hat, George Ella from Harlan,
Barbara, Leatha, Robert, Rita,
Chris, Jonathan, Jack, George,
Gurney, Michael, Jeff Daniel, Glenn,
Marie, Elizabeth, Dana, Denise,
Sidney, Sharyn, Lee, Silas,
Phyllis, Jo, Pat, June
— we'll *all* do the dishes for words.

ANNA EGAN SMUCKER
Bridgeport, WV

Talking Perry County kinfolks around the dinner table. Laughing over mountain-raised men with soapsuds to their elbows, taking their turn washing supper dishes. Harmonizing "Amazing Grace" at midnight out on the front porch. Taking good-natured ribbing for sitting-in on a video class and not even owning a video camera. Sounds more like a visit back home, doesn't it? I think that's why so many of us keep going back. And being able to keep in mind always Mr. Still's words: "Listen to the people around you — pay attention to what they do. Write what you know about."

NORMA RAMSEY EVERSOLE
Rockcastle County, KY

❧ LANDMARK ❧
HARRIETTE ARNOW

Times and places were mingled in my head; the past was part of the present, close as the red cedar water bucket in the kitchen.... My people loved the past more than their present lives, I think, but it cannot be said that we lived in the past. Two things tied all time together: these had run through most of the old stories to shape the lives of men, and so did they shape our lives and the lives of the people about us. These were the land and the Cumberland.

— HARRIETTE ARNOW

from Tracing Trips to Hindman

My first trip to the Hindman Settlement School Writers Workshop was in 1986, the year Harriette Arnow died. Mike Mullins invited me to come and speak as a part of the Arnow Memorial program, at least partly because Jim Wayne Miller knew I was writing my dissertation about *Hunter's Horn* and planning to be her biographer. It was a hot day in July — the main hall wasn't air conditioned back then. All the ceiling fans were whirling, and everybody was sweating and fanning. But some of the heat I felt was generated by my own excitement....

I've attended part or all of most of the other workshops ever since then. The first year I went as a student. My purpose was to interview Harriette's former students and to attend Jim Wayne Miller's Appalachian Literature class, which I took several more times, and my own teaching has been better for it. I appreciated the mobile filing cabinet that was Jim Wayne's car — he repeatedly shared with me notes and correspondence and clippings about Harriette Arnow. One of my favorite things he gave me is a photocopy of the outline of her hand, drawn by James Still, who didn't have a camera but instead had the habit of making a memento by tracing the hand of a person who came to visit him. He had Harriette to sign the tracing. She dated it August 9, 1961, and he wrote along the top of the page, "The hand that wrote *The Dollmaker.*"

SANDRA L. BALLARD
Boone, NC

Doing Dishes with Harriette

In olden days, before air conditioning, before Vulcan, that stainless steel automatic dishwasher, came to the Settlement School, back when the kitchen was between the dining room and the Great Hall, there was a six-sink, face-to-face dish room (two rows of three, joined at the faucets) where everybody — Harriette Arnow & Cratis Williams, Jim Wayne Miller & Joyce Hancock, everybody as far as I know but Mr. Still — plunged hands in soapsuds, scrubbed pot vessels, lowered wire baskets of plates, cups, and silverware into the scalding rinse, and then lifted them onto the drainboard. It was about a million degrees in there. And dishwashing is always hot work. Thus Vulcan.

Sometimes we sang, usually hymns. Hymns are good for a sense of solidarity and fulfilling your duty by suffering for others. Sometimes we shared stories and jokes and dreams of the day.

But on the nights when Harriette and Harold Arnow were part of the dish team, we didn't need to entertain ourselves. We had them.

Harriette didn't hear well in a quiet room. The dish room, with its clanging and swoshing and clattering, must have been torture for her. So any exchange between husband and wife on dish duty had to be loud. It followed a pattern, too. She was usually irritated over something — and he was amused. Or she was accusatory about something — and he was innocent. Or she was right about something — and he was right, too. He was right there with her.

Harriette was very small. I'm 5'2" and I felt tall around Harriette. Her gray-white energetic hair was straight and cut close, except for a few waves around her face. She wore dark-rimmed glasses, a little large and slightly crooked, through which her blue-gray eyes pierced the world. Most often she wore a straight cotton shirtwaist dress with a tie or self-belt and no jewelry. The first time I heard her read, four years before I came to Hindman, I was eight months pregnant, gigantic and awestruck, and all I managed to say to her was, "*The Dollmaker* is so huge and you're so small!" I expect she had heard that before, but she didn't let on. Neither did she spend any words to ransom my literal-mindedness.

Harriette was a no-frills no-nonsense person, a driven person, where-as Harold played the fool for us, dancing around his over-burdened wife. I don't mean this was her attitude. I mean she literally (literarily) carried the heaviest load of anybody in those frontier workshop days because folks didn't send manuscripts in by June 1 as they do now.

Nobody sorted and mailed them out to the staff in early July so we had time to read and prepare comments before we gathered. Oh, no. After Sunday night sandwiches, salutations, and snake-warnings, we met in Mike's office and he handed those suckers out. It was daunting enough to get sixteen whole poetry manuscripts — there were no page limits in those days either — but Harriette got entire novels: a wheel-barrow full. Hand-typed, often with a gray, dry ribbon, for this was before computers. And she took these tomes, which no doubt out-weighed her — to her apartment on the ground floor of the May Stone Building, below the kitchen and across from the laundry room, and she read every word. She made notes, wrote out comments, prepared for conferences. She must have sometimes stayed up all night.

So, when conference time came, if the writer revealed himself to be lazy or a dabbler, someone who wasn't going to take and use the advice Harriette had put so much of herself into, she was probably mad as hell at him. But she didn't show it. She saved it. For Harold and the dish room. All of us do this, of course: let loose on loved ones the ire we don't direct at its source. Harold probably did it, too, at home. But in public, for our benefit, this was their routine: Harriette saw what was wrong with the world and Harold saw what was right. Like Jack Sprat and his wife, they parceled things out, divided them up.

And so, between the two of them, they washed the dishes clean.

GEORGE ELLA LYON
Lexington, KY

from A Letter by Joyce Ann Hancock*

*(sent to Sandy Ballard September 14, 1997,
accompanying a photograph of Harriette Arnow)*

"I regret that I didn't take more pictures of her when I had the chance.

"I'll tell you one little story she told me while we were walking together that same morning after striking her image, as we used to say, before breakfast. It was about six or seven, the day was bright and Mr. Still had just presented Ms. Arnow with a freshly cut rose from his garden. He did it with some gallantry, I must say. I love the way these people respect and love each other. And she'd picked up that apple for our walk.

"We're walking over Troublesome Creek Bridge (North Fork, of course) and chatting. At that time I worked in Berea as the Director or Participants Coordinator (my titles seemed to shift, but I have never paid much mind to titles) and of course Harriette Arnow related with no small distaste the days when she was a student at Berea College. In those days, she told me, with irritation, us girls were not allowed to walk down the same sidewalk as the boys. Clearly Ms. Arnow was way too free a spirit for the times in which she'd been born."

She included an extra photo and wrote "Am sending you a little extra gift, just because I sense a kindredness with you."

"If you know of others who need photos of almost any Appa-lachian writer, I am sitting here in my house with pictures of them. And if I can be of any other use to you — I want to support your work, English teacher to English teacher — I'm right here."

---

*After Berea, Joyce moved to Louisville to teach at Jefferson Community College and sent this letter to Sandy Ballard from her home at 3315 Richard Avenue. Joyce and her cat Dude perished on the night of December 3, 1997, as the result of a house fire. After the 1997 workshop, she gave Hindman a scrapbook containing photo-graphs she took at the workshops she attended. [JG]

The Pink Umbrella
(for Joyce Ann Hancock)

I picked it up from its resting place, in the basket next to my front door.

I take it to the mailbox on rainy days, with me, to get the day's deposit.

That scarred, blackened appearance will not seem to wash off.

And it still has the horrible smell that only comes from something that has been burned and then wettened.

I think I must want that smell to remain — to remind me of the terrible tragedy.

When I opened the box from the auction, the box of what I thought was books — upon examining the bottom of the box, I found the pink umbrella.

I was amazed at how remarkably intact it was — considering the whole house had been gutted by fire.

Luckily, I got a few of those things that remind me of her — of her smiling face.

I think she is at peace now — and I know she never was, here — with us, and as we approach the anniversary of her death, I want you to remember Joyce Ann and all the good wishes she had for all of us.

I wish for each of you a pink umbrella.

MARY ANN CARRICO-Mitchell
Campbellsburg, KY

from Stories of the Leaf Writers

In the same way as family and home, Hindman is a haunted place for me: the shadow of the man whose spirit informs its every aspect, Jim Wayne Miller, lingers in the back of every room always, and Harriette Arnow, Cratis Williams, Al Stewart, and James Still feature prominently in the collective memory of the place.

All the writers I've mentioned, plus many, many more, have stood in the front of the great hall, with those beautiful quilts hanging as backdrop, and given amazing readings that made us laugh until we cried and cry until we laughed at ourselves. Once when Wilma Dykeman was reading, Harold and Harriette Arnow, both of whom were hard of hearing, were sitting in the front row — Harriette was fixed with rapt attention on Wilma. But Harold was trying to "whisper" to her that he needed the key to return to the apartment. "Be quiet, Harold," she hissed in the loudest whisper humanly possible, "people are reading." Everyone collapsed in giggles, covering their faces with their hands, while Wilma, who had to have heard every word, soldiered on, straight-faced and on task.

Harold was an old newspaper man and he came to the workshop to be with Harriette, to socialize with all the interesting people, and to flirt innocently with all the ladies. Harriette was there in service to the written word. And for a week each summer—so are we all.

RITA QUILLEN
Gate City, VA

VII

SINGING ON THE HILL

Hindman Magic — Three Eras

I've been attending the Appalachian Writers Workshop at Hindman Settlement School every summer for more than twenty years now and I'd like to try to sum up what makes it so magical.

I think the workshop can be divided into three eras: the Harriette Arnow era, the Jim Wayne Miller era, and the Lee Smith era. Of course that is not precise. There have been overlaps and a few years have not even featured one of these dominant personalities, but I do think this breakdown works. What is ironic is that despite the very different personalities of these, they all three sustained a spirit that defines the workshop. In a word, I think the dominant spirit is egalitarian.

Harriette Arnow was unabashed in her support for the political left and philosophically she believed in equality — and this belief stamped her participation. From the beginning, the Hindman Workshop was a place where "faculty" and "students" mixed and shared. In the Arnow era, the noun/verb "swarp" was adopted to describe the unique happenings that enlivened the Workshop after hours. Our "swarps" included just plain flat-out partying, but that was enlivened periodically by spontaneous poetry readings and bursts into song — both solo and group — and, yes, even diatribes! Sometimes the porch group would be in "plenary session," with all riveted upon a single "performer," then, quite easily, the dynamic would change to little sub-groups or even pairs. Harriette Arnow herself was usually sipping Old Granddad and smoking Lucky Strikes in her room while this was happening, but other faculty would join the students, and she was there in spirit.

When Harriette died, many wondered if the Workshop could survive without a big-name author like herself, but Jim Wayne Miller was a compelling personality, quite charismatic in his own way. And, man, could Jim Wayne "swarp" with the best of them! Again, when Jim Wayne died, some doubted the future of the workshop, but Lee Smith shares the generosity and faith in nascent writers that Arnow and Miller stamped upon the Workshop as its signature trait. And she combines much of the national reputation that Arnow enjoyed with many of the people skills that made Miller so popular. During her era, for the first time, the porch has been joined by the parlor, and the Hindman Workshop After Hours has enjoyed a dual foci. The parlor is for singing (since Rita Quillen first stepped foot in Knott County this has been one of the Workshop's great strengths), but adjacent is the kitchen and the deck for those who want to be within earshot but also enjoy a conversation or two. Smith, like Arnow, isn't always present, but, again, her spirit is there and her fellow faculty often enjoy both crowds or at least one.

The swarp is central to the Hindman Workshop. We come to Hindman to sing, to read our creative work, and to converse. It is a place where many of the faculty were Hindman students once and where everyone works and plays together as equals.

GEORGE BROSI
Berea, KY

———————

For such a wordful place, what I remember most about Hindman is the music. After a day and a night of writing, my head absolutely filled with words laid longway, sideway, crossway, anyway. I would come of an evening through the dark following sound yearning out of windows and set up on chairs on the backporch. Fiddle and harp disassemble my tumble of words, until they lay nicely in chords hung loose around my hips. The rise and fall of my friends' voices breathed me clean of too much wordfulness and slipped me into the river of longing, looking, eventually, for the other shore.

LEE HOWARD
Portland, OR

Songmaker: Metaphor for Rita

Picking her way
'cross slides and sharp ridges,
the alto of a long, yellow hound,
eyes on the hot running fox,
melds with the soprano pack
that bells the high reaches.
It carries down the mountain,
mellows the chorus,
gilds the night.

JIM HINSDALE
Tryon, NC

from Stories of the Leaf Writers

Lots of memories involve singing. In recent years Betty Smith and Deborah Thompson, the angel and the troubadour, lead the nightly singing in Apt. 2 in the "Cliff apartments." In years past, we always gathered on the front porch up on the Preece dorm, but as we're all getting older, we've seemed to stay down at a lower elevation lately!

Speaking of that front porch gathering place, there's several memorable stories tied to it. While Hindman's a very sedate, well-behaved workshop compared to many I've heard about, occasionally someone does imbibe a bit. Ed McClanahan passed out cold in mid-sentence during one of our porch singalongs, falling like a buckshot duck out of his straight chair onto the floor of the porch without so much as a flinch, nearly scaring onlookers into a cardiac arrest. He wasn't hurt — and after regaining consciousness a minute later, to every one's delight, simply returned to his chair and finished his story. That's the way it is at the Appalachian Writer's Workshop; nothing gets in the way of the story.

RITA QUILLEN
Gate City, VA

Tribal Dance at the Appalachian Writers Workshop

There's no morning dance on the spider-webbed
bridge, no troubling creek dance of minnows
giggling below mist, & no cigarette smoke
swirling from a picnic table, encouraging
the sun, as if it were a young writer.

No phalanx of rocking chairs pumping time
like pistons in the engine of early light.
It's not a dance cars did covered in dew
or sweat of the road. No prancing pens
in the classes. No saraband of chatter & scribble.

The dance, when it comes, is not the wine
of music, the whiskey of bodies twirling,
nor the beer of memory. It is all of this
in the prison of hills, under guard
of the trees that came here decades
& centuries ago & waited for us.

RON HOUCHIN
Huntington, WV

On the Floor of Apartment 2

I have lived away from Appalachia for far too long. So I knew exactly what Robert Morgan was talking about when he told the short-story class at the Appalachian Writers Workshop this past summer that he had made himself a student of Appalachia out of homesickness and nostalgia. Morgan moved to Cornell in the 1970s. I moved to Houston, Texas, in the summer of 1977 — the year the AWW began at Hindman.

I went to the workshop for the first time during a visit home to Elizabethton, Tennessee, in the summer of 2001. It was a homecoming unlike any other. What transported me back to the mountains most was the music, especially the late-evening gatherings with Betty Smith, Steve Lyon, Deborah Thompson, and other fine musicians.

I fell in love with folk music in high school and with mountain ballads sung by Jean Ritchie when I was a student at East Tennessee State University. I learned many of the traditional songs and even learned to play the dulcimer. On my first night in Apartment 2, I was happily tearful as I sat on the floor, singing along with the group. Betty's dulcimer and her clear, Appalachian voice gave expression to mournful ballads I hadn't heard since college. And it was as if the angel band had come to welcome me home when we all sang the perfect little hymn "Simple Gifts" in the lunch line at Hindman.

As one who has lived too far away for too long, I can vouch for the truth of Robert Morgan's dictum that sometimes we writers have to put distance between ourselves and a place before we can write about it. Winter is approaching, and this morning the first norther swept out of an ominous Texas sky. But I feel anchored solid as I think of the settlement on Troublesome Creek and the "fair and tender ladies" of Appalachian song.

ANN SHURGIN
Waller, TX

Hindman

To come to the Appalachian Writers Workshop at Hindman is to come home to a place where people understand you. I am a New Yorker whose first job was in eastern Kentucky where I was deeply touched by the people I knew. I must have swallowed too much of the Kentucky River for eastern Kentucky remains an important part of my being. This makes for something of a split personality....

There are so many great moments in my four summers at Hindman it is hard to know which to relate....

Not all of the satisfactions are in the use of words: just as vital connections are made through music. Imagine the famous banjo player Lee Sexton, and the excellent fiddler Ray Sloan among others playing while we square-danced the length of the great room — in my case tangling up the whole set. It didn't matter. The joy of it.... Not to mention Betty Smith and the evenings up the hill where people can bring their instruments and sing powerful songs like "Angel Band" and "Silver Dagger." For somebody who thrives on literature and old time music and is even a closet fiddle player, I was in my element the whole time... If you want a place to grow in your work among people who understand you, go to Hindman. I have kept this a secret because I don't want the Appalachian Writers Conference to get too big.

NOEL SMITH
Pomona, NY

How Writers Find Their Groove

No stereo, so Gurney
nosed his truck to Stuckey's porch
and cranked up WMMT
for an hour or so until
they drank the battery dry,
then Jim waltzed on with Peggy
to his own good baritone
one-two-threeing in a lower key,
words maybe not the same
as the radio played, but
that was okay, they could dance
to it, and one little piece
of night, perfect with things they
loved, could go on forever
so long as Jim kept singing.

DANA S. WILDSMITH
Bethlehem, GA

———————

It was 2 a.m. Sunday night, or more aptly put, Monday Morning Hindman Settlement Appalachian Writing Workshop Time, and on my way out of apartment 2 upstairs, first dorm on the hill, I spotted a trail of cookie crumbs and droplets of milk leading to a hunched and "wizened" figure sitting on the top step of the staircase.

I intended to skip out for morning air. I stepped around him and noticed he was intently reading, his concentration unbroken by my weight on the steps. Later during a communal lunch I made an effort to meet him and he introduced himself as Harry Dean. We exchanged pleasantries and he asked me if I had signed up for the afternoon open readings, and if so, what day? He mentioned the spots were going fast.

Next time I saw him, he was Betty's able sidekick in an every-night mountain music jam session singing and playing, among other songs, "A Man of Constant Sorrow" with ever increasing assuredness as Steve led out with his picking and singing after a hardly recognizable pause to allow Betty to set the piece. Nights to remember, I'm sure!

FRED TARR
Ft. Thomas, KY

Something Ancient
(*Journal Entry, August 1, 2001*)

I am sitting by Troublesome Creek. In my spot next to the bridge where I pitched my tent two years ago. I stayed in a tent that year because we were too broke to afford both tuition and boarding. Nothing could keep me from coming to Hindman, though. And I wanted to stay in a tent. It wasn't just because we were low on cash that year. I liked having nothing more than the tent fabric between me and the summer air; I could hear the creek flowing all night, and it was a great comfort to me. I could hear the katydids and cicadas and all the night sounds of this place. It was the best sleep I have ever had.

It's morning and stripes of mist lie on the ridges. The air smells like leaves and creek-water. The place is coming awake and I can hear the women coming off the mountain from Preece. Their laughter echoes down to me. Men are walking down from the Cliffside Apartments. We will all file into the dining hall and have breakfast together. Betty will have us sing first, a song of thanks. It is my turn to wash dishes.

We were talking last night about how the Settlement School is an ancient place. We all feel like something happened here long ago that binds us together. Whatever it was, it made us family. It is a kinship we can't explain, but we know it exists. There is a pulsing in the land here, like a big bloodline that we all share. When I am here, I am among not only friends, but family. It seems I can sing in harmony better with people here. We are able to have good conversations because we don't have to fill in the gaps — we know easily what the other means. We danced on the porch last night and we all knew how the other was going to move; it was as if we had rehearsed our steps for many years together. It is amazing to me that every year I meet people here whom I feel as if I have known all of my life. Maybe it is because we are all so similar — most of us are not only creative people, but Appalachians, too. And even those who are not Appalachians have mountain souls.

There is something about this place. Something magic happened here once. And it still does. For one week out of the year, things happen here that can't be explained. Like the way I was able to finish my novel last night, as if everybody here had some hand in what I was writing. And the way we depend on each other and support one another. When I need a prayer, or good thoughts, or whatever, I go to my Hindman friends first. Because we operate like a family. These people are my brothers and sisters. We are connected by something ancient, something that we can't put a name to.

SILAS HOUSE
Lily, KY

———————

The Winds of the Past
(A Song)

The times are now past and the days are gone by;
Their shadows like clouds seem to drift 'cross the sky;
And down through the valley and up through the cove
The winds of the past still whisper and rove;
And down through the valley and up through the cove
The winds of the past still whisper and rove.

The wild seas roll on and the high hills abide;
The strong hand of God still steadies the tide;
Small birds still murmur in green shady groves,
The raven's wings dip as the wide skies he roves.
And down through the valley and up through the cove.
The winds of the past still whisper and rove.

The joys of those lost days we try to recall,
Old friends are best though the whole world should fall;
The cold nights of terror we forgive and forget,
And cherish the sound of the song singing yet.
And down through the valley and up through the cove,
The winds of the past still whisper and rove.

Man in his passion still rants and he raves.
Heroes in battle still go to their graves;
Leaves in the fall still change red and gold,
Winter comes 'round and the wind still blows cold.
And down through the valley and up through the cove,
The winds of the past still whisper and rove.

Some sons of farmer still cherish the soil,
Though in the city they've taken up toil;
The hunter still hunts and the fishermen fish,
The dreamer still counts on a star for his wish.
And down through the valley and up through the cove,
The winds of the past still whisper and rove.

BETTY SMITH
Hot Springs, NC

VIII

PORCH STORIES

On the Porch at Preece: Nightfall

for Ron Rash

'cause I want to get right with God
— *Lucinda Williams*

Stomp and thump
ringed the porch,
our stage of praise
to the night, the glory
hallelujah of words.

Shout that amen, brother!
Wave those arms, sister!

We sing the wild hymns
the ancient redemption tale,
dance the healing steps
the sounds beating
down on us like rain.
Our stories carry over the mountain
baptizing all who will listen.

MARIANNE WORTHINGTON
Williamsburg, KY

A Place Called Hindman Settlement School

In the cool of the evening on the porch at Stuckey House, I lean my cane-bottomed chair against the wall. To my right is a deep gulch where ferns and Rose of Sharon bushes are growing. A stream meanders its way to Troublesome. The road to Isom is filled with clacking traffic.

Just over the rise, to my left, I can see buildings on Main Street. In front of me, is the May Stone building framed between walnut and hemlock trees. It's quiet there because this is Friday and most of the writers have gone to Wolfpen Creek to see Mr. James Still's homeplace. Only Carol and I remain, writing in companionable solitude, sipping Evian water now and then, as we listen to bird songs and smell old cigarette butts in the week-old ashtray.

RUTH ANN ANTLE
Russell Springs, KY

Lauds
(Hindman, KY, August 1, 2001)

on the western side of an eastern mountain
in the near side of early morning

before a beam can clear the peak
boulders huddle in the chill night stream

wait for light to insinuate time
between branches of pine like smoke

drifts from a kitchen chimney like a certain
fragrance of coffee and toast lifts curtain lace

like a thumb ruffles pages of a worn book
to look for a verse to inform the day

ELIZABETH JOHNSON
Madisonville, KY

Porch Life

Rockers come in pairs
like missionaries,
in multiples of two
like survivors brought
off Noah's Ark,

no two identical
even though experts
can't identify differences
causing twins to walk
at different speeds.

Pairs come equipped with
porch-floor connectors
allowing occupants
to communicate through
arms, backs, wicker seats;

thoughts pass to and fro
using energy left over
from lightning bugs,
katydids, cat purrs,
mosquito concerts.
Parts people don't
even know they
possess reach out
and quietly heal
each other's troubles.
Watch our rockers
wave good-bye
as we walk
arm in arm
into the future.

GLENN MCKEE
Waterville, ME

A Conversation with James Still

It was a beautiful balmy Hindman afternoon. I was sitting alone in one of the rockers on the front porch of the May Stone Building, eyes shut, basking in the warmth of the sun and the helpful comments I had just received during the conference on my short story. I may even have been dozing a little.

One of the other rockers creaked, and I was aware that I was no longer alone. I opened my eyes to see James Still lowering himself into the chair closest to mine. It was my first year at the Appalachian Writers

Workshop, and I had never before been so near this great American writer. I was tongue-tied.

"Didn't mean to wake you up," he said. "Where're you from?" He glanced at my name tag.

"Prestonsburg for the past twenty-eight years," I answered, "but I've just retired and moved back home to Somerset."

We chatted for a few minutes about mutual acquaintances. I was surprised and happy to discover that he knew some of the people I'd taught with at Prestonsburg Community College. Soon, however, he changed the subject, and I listened with rapt attention. He didn't talk about books or writing, but rather about his experiences as a soldier during World War II. He spoke of his tour of duty in Africa, and of his traveling to other countries, particularly Egypt, while he was there. He recounted his fascination with the pyramids and the ruins of the temples of the pharaohs. He remembered the names of fellow soldiers and spoke of them as though he'd seen them only yesterday. The humanity which is so characteristic of Mr. Still's writing about his neighbors on Troublesome Creek was rich in his voice that day as he talked about these men, far from home, with whom he'd shared good times and bad.

After about an hour others joined us on the porch, and Mr. Still began talking with some of them. I sat quietly, thinking of what he had said, and feeling privileged that he had shared these thoughts with me. In some small way I felt I knew the men he had described, that we now had more mutual friends between us. And that's what great writers do. It was James Still's gift to me that day, just as his gift to the world was in the characters he made real and the stories he told.

I've returned to Hindman many times since then, but that special afternoon with James Still remains for me the essence of the Appalachian Writers Workshop.

LAURA WEDDLE
Somerset, KY

The Porch

At dusk on the porch we rock and talk
on Friday night with most people gone.
One tells of the threat from a dog on a walk.
Another laughs at the oats she's sown.

Another one waits at the door for the phone.
Then someone points up the hill at a hawk
as it sails through the trees austere and alone.
Like us, it seeks a truth it can stalk.

HARRY DEAN
Cleveland, TN

Porching

An open chord porch
exclamations of fireflies and mosquitoes
affirm delicate word-shape
and tuned silences between
stories, laughter and songs

DORY L. HUDSPETH
Alvaton, KY

Hindman Memories

That first day had been hot and muggy, and a group began to gather listlessly on the front porch, relishing the coolness of a starry Kentucky night. After we'd exchanged names and hometowns, I turned to Theodosia Barrett, who was from Lebanon, Virginia and the only person there I'd met before, and asked what she was working on.

"Well," she drawled, "right now I'm working on a story about Abner Vance."

"Abner Vance!" squealed Adda Davis, who was from Paynesville, West Virginia. "That's who I'm working on!" They started right in comparing notes.

"My word," I thought. "How could two writers totally unknown to each other and separated by miles have chosen to write on the same subject?"

This started the ball rolling, and the crescendo of voices rose accordingly, especially when Mabel Wyrick began trying to convince us that her title, "Factual Folklore," was not an oxymoron.

We finally took ourselves off to bed but resumed the talkfest over coffee before 6:00 a.m., much to the displeasure of our roommates who shushed us grumpily. I have since come to realize that the Hindman experience is a collage of such occurrences.

RUTH TRIMBLE
Kingsport, TN

Augury

Drifting out of the night like a pale green piece
of the August moon,
a luna moth crashes our party,
fastens itself to the wall; and all at once, the yellow glow
on the porch comes from a bare bulb
mounted beside the screen door;
the night presses in around us;
we can smell the dirt, the pungent weeds,
the crowded trees on the surrounding hillsides
have moved toward us secretly
like the treacherous woods
that brought down Macbeth.
And all of us are suddenly separate,
though we continue to sing and talk
as we had just a moment before.
Big as a child's hand widespread, this emissary
must be a warning —
we are not the wall,
nor the woods around us;
we're not the wine we're drinking.
This ghost of a leaf, thin as paper,
is a note pinned to the door.

EDWINA PENDARVIS
Huntington, WV

Wild Call

The dark scatters out
Through hemlock and pine
As dawn slips over
    the mountain
I watch
Blue haze of ridges
       Marching
West and a hawk soaring
       Wheeling
Red tail flashing
        Gliding
He circles
       Down
Over the cabin,
     Calls once and
I leave with him.

VADA JOHNSON
Radcliff, KY

❧ LANDMARK ❧

JIM WAYNE MILLER

Harvest (excerpt)

So he wasn't sad to see his life gathered
up in books, kept on a shelf like dry seeds
in an envelope, or carried far off
like spanish needles in a fox's fur.
His people brought the salt sea in their songs;
now they moved mountains to the cities
and made all love and death and sorrow sweet there.

Heaviness was always left behind
to perish, to topple like a stone chimney.

But what was lightest lasted, lived in song.

— JIM WAYNE MILLER

Keeping Watch

in memory of Jim Wayne Miller

This man who slept in his clothes
changed in deeper ways,
unshed trousers and shirt the camouflage
under which he transformed
into briers, oak trees, panthers.
His lidded eyes grew powerful,
his thoughts the red
of fresh meat.

At 4 a.m.
he burst from himself
to hunt the woods
like an owl,
the blood of mice and shrews
brilliant on his lips.

Late for breakfast
at the workshop,
he sat down at table
like a pilgrim or prophet
and spoke over eggs
a strange blessing.

Now
he is lost to us, vanished
among tanagers
and weevils, mayflies
and small upland trout.

Jim Wayne Miller   159

Gone as the clouds that
scud eastward, far from here,
toward his homeplace.
Now chickadees wear
his best shirt. Now
every gray and hungover dawn
smells like him
just finished with a smoke.

RICHARD HAGUE
Cincinnati, OH

———————

Jim Wayne was a close friend as well as a Gnomon author and many
memories I have of him are at Hindman. At evening gatherings he was
barely legal (or illegal) chain-smoking in doorways. He seemed to almost
never sleep and was caught more than once asleep at the wheel of his
parked car, a car whose trunk served as an extra faculty office, library,
and bookstore. Jim Wayne also had a special parking place up the hill,
now close to where James Still is laid to rest. Jim Wayne was always
encouraging young authors, always making connections — some from
left field, comparing aspects of Appalachian literature with what was
happening in German literature back in the 19th century. Jim Wavne
was the behind-the-scenes power broker of the workshop and often it
was with his recommendation that Mike hired faculty.

JONATHAN GREENE
Franklin County, KY

———————

In Remembrance

The trucks still roll, Jim Wayne.
Create intermittent thunder, like
a maul driving wedges to split
pre-dawn tranquility.

As I walked where we walked,
I could almost see you,
coffee cup in hand, hurrying
to an early conference.

Because you were not here, dear friend,
the apple tree bore no fruit,
and the kudzu did not bloom
in Knott County....

RUTH TRIMBLE
Kingsport, TN

Still Listening

My interest in learning about the literature and heritage of Appalachia
was the reason I first attended the Hindman Settlement School's Appalachian Writers Workshop. The 1987 afternoon sessions, led by Dr. Jim
Wayne Miller, quickly convinced me the term "Appalachian scholar"
was no oxymoron. His enthusiasm and global vision (plus his trunk
filled with books) served as a catalyst for my interest in unearthing and

promoting the true image of one oddly-shaped piece of the Appalachian region's "outer rim," Wild Wonderful West Virginia.

Miller became my mentor, an Obi Wan Kanobi, as I set out to research and write about the little-known multicultural literary history of West Virginia and the true nature of the state's culture and heritage.

Taking his humor as a guide, I coined an acronym, PIWASH, to represent the image held by many flatlanders regarding the inhabitants of West Virginia. Outsiders are often convinced we are PIWASH: poor, illiterate, white, Anglo-shoeless hillbillies who live somewhere in the mountains near Richmond.

In the last letter I received from Jim Wayne, dated one month before his death, he told me of his intention to wear his PIWASH tee-shirt as often as possible and his glee at explaining the word, especially to students.

Miller loved to recount humorous classroom happenings. One of his favorite quotes, the result of a visit to a high school classroom were these words spoken by a boy to his teacher, "It was hard not to listen to him."

The boy was ABSOLUTELY right. It was impossible not to listen to him. We are still listening.

PHYLLIS WILSON MOORE
Clarksburg, WV

———

Brier Leaves Hindman, Kentucky
(August 1996)

Ad in *Troublesome Creek Times:*
Wanted, particular occupant for bench
at May Stone Dining Hall. Applicant
must be gregarious, sagacious, erudite,
pedagogically perfect, raconteur
of the first order. Superior writing
skills, wry humor, and acute
sense of the absurd a must.
Apply immediately, bench is lonely.

JANE HICKS
Blountville, TN

How rare and amazing Jim Wayne's energy, his humor, his mind, his
passion for the southern Appalachian region, its culture and people. His
light burned so brightly and touched so many, I could not imagine such
fire ever being extinguished. In June 1996, Danny and I attended a special birthday celebration for Mr. Still, his ninetieth. Jim Wayne was on
the dais, ready to offer his tribute to Mr. Still. When he rose to speak,
everyone gasped. We knew about the cancer, but were not prepared for
this. Here was a Jim Wayne we hardly recognized, so small and gaunt,
battling for every breath, yet he finished his talk through sheer force of
will. We visited him privately in his room after the speeches were given.
He let Danny and me sit beside him on the bed and took our hands. We
all knew it was the last time we would meet, but said nothing of that.
Jim Wayne seemed glad that Danny and I were happy together, that I

was taking good care of his old friend. We have often thought of that day, when we felt closest to Jim, the day of our sweetest and last good-bye.

LINDA PARSONS MARION
Knoxville, TN

In my dream I see Jim Wayne sitting in a stuffed armchair tilted sideways in the clouds. He is his old self: vigorous, urbane, glittering with wit and words. He lifts his right hand in a wave or a blessing, then smiles and says, "Wake me when God wakes."

GEORGE ELLA LYON
Lexington, KY

Tobacco Love
(In Memorium Jim Wayne Miller)

I had loved her so long,
my hand always caressing

her slender white gloved arm,
our breath always mingling intimacy

no wonder she finally loved me back
with an all-consuming flame.

JONATHAN GREENE
Franklin County, KY

IX

HINDMAN WORLDWIDE

In Hind(man) Sight

Hindman — What is it if not a paradox of the Holy Land and the Hollywood of Appalachian Writers? The word there is gospel; and who of us at the workshop hasn't sought an autograph?

I experienced first-hand a vision of Jesse's *Trees of Heaven,* I reflected beside James' "Still" waters, and I walked in the actual footsteps of the "Fair and Tender" Lady herself, Lee Smith. Silas was in the "House," and in hearing his reading of his then unpublished work I knew that there was "gold in them there hills"— a thousand miles away from California. Among my people was an understanding conveyed with or without words, but mercy, when words were used it was miraculous!

SANDI KEATON-WILSON
Edmonton, KY

Repairing to Hindman

In the climactic scene of Ray Bradbury's classic science-fiction novel, *Fahrenheit 451,* there is a powerfully understated but unforgettable encounter between the protagonist, Guy Montag, a fugitive, and an encamped gathering of book-lovers. Montag comes upon them gathered around a campfire beside a stream in a remote and wooded country place.

In this futuristic story, first published in 1953, Montag is in flight from a totalitarian society in which all books are banned, the better to maintain complete control of the populace in the interest of "national security." The primary role of local fire departments is to find and destroy secret caches of books — pile them up and torch them to ashes. (The novel's title refers to the temperature at which book paper catches fire and burns.) Montag, a fireman, finally rebels against his destructive role and flees into the countryside, where he is welcomed into a community of readers, a unit within the national underground resistance movement.

After years on the run, the men and women of the resistance have perfected the one and only way they can ensure the safety of their books: by memorizing them. They have developed photographic memories, and each is responsible for preserving a major work of literature or the entire works of a chosen author. Thus, "Jonathan Swift" recites *Gulliver's Travels,* and *The Origin of the Species* comes from "Charles Darwin," and "Tom Paine" is there, along with "Lincoln" and "Jefferson" and "Henry David Thoreau." If you want to "read" *Moby Dick* or *A Tale of Two Cities* — or, presumably, *Native Son* or *Little Women* or *A Child's Garden of Verses* — you go and sit at the feet of the one who knows the book by heart.

For some reason I can't explain, the writers workshop at Hindman always comes to mind when I think about that scene from the Bradbury novel. Perhaps there is a physical connection; in the movie version of *Fahrenheit 451,* the colony of readers lives among wooded hills above a meandering stream, and gathers in the evenings for dinner and conversation and "readings." It would seem only natural that one among them might well stand and deliver *The Dollmaker* or *River of Earth* or *Oral History.* And there is perhaps a more philosophical explanation as well.

As with the remnant colony in Bradbury's story, the writers workshop at Hindman is about the preservation and perpetuation of literature, and the nurture of writers and readers, and the encouragement of all who gather there to keep the faith and fight to the end against a culture that seems increasingly hostile to independent thinking and to strong feelings put down on paper.

The annual Appalachian gathering of writers is an association of people in a familiar haunt. Whether we have entered that circle only once or twice, or every August for a quarter-century, we repair to Hindman. As in the very definition of that rarely heard verb, the act of going is likened to a return to one's homeland.

Something there is about rockers on the porch, table talk in the dining hall, words and music and laughter in the evening air. And old friends returning, and others absent but never out of mind. Hindman is more than a place; it's a spirit.

JOHN EGERTON
Nashville, TN

Appalachian Writers Workshop
(First Year at Hindman Settlement School, August, 1978)

....By Wednesday I was so tired I didn't even go to lunch. I told Albert that I was going to my room to rest awhile before starting my afternoon round of conferences with individual writers. I didn't mean to actually go to sleep, but as soon as I hit the mattress I conked out. When I woke up it was nearly 2 p.m. Hastening down the hill I saw a clutch of people standing outside the dining hall with odd looks on their faces. Before I could ask what was going on, Albert took me aside. He was clearly agitated. He said the U.S. State Department had been there, two men and one woman. They were escorting a poet and cultural activist from the Faroe Islands in the North Atlantic where the islanders were struggling to break free of Denmark's colonial influence. Someone had suggested that the poet might find the Appalachian region interesting, so a trip to the Writers Workshop at Hindman became a primary destination.

Somewhere along the way the poet had got hold of a copy of my new book, *Kinfolks*. He wanted to meet the author.

"We'd like to see Mr. Norman," the head fed said. "We were told he was here."

"He's here, but he's in his room resting right now," Albert replied.

"We need to see him. Could someone go get him?"

"No," said Albert. "He asked not to be disturbed."

"But it's on our agenda. It's a priority."

Albert said, "It might be your priority, but my priority is not to disturb Mr. Norman."

The government man brought himself up to his full height. Looking down at Albert who looked back defiantly, the government official said, "Sir, do you realize that we're from the State Department?"

Albert said, "Listen here. I don't care who you are or where you're from. You ain't no more to me than one of these Knott County deputy sheriffs. Mr. Norman doesn't want to be disturbed and that's the way it's going to be."

Albert prevailed. The State Department retreated. Fortunately, later in the afternoon, they came back and I had a chance to visit with them. The poet from the Faroe Islands turned out to be extremely engaging. Standing on the bridge, looking down at the water, we talked together for a good half-hour. Earlier, having had no lunch, I had picked up a hunk of bread and put it in my leather shoulder bag which in those days I always carried. As our visit was coming to an end, on impulse I reached into my bag, pulled out my bread and started throwing pieces of it into Troublesome Creek. Then I handed the bread to the poet. He threw pieces into the water until he had no more.

"Bread upon the waters," he said. I looked at him and nodded. We both grinned. The State Department and Albert Stewart had done better jobs than they knew.

GURNEY NORMAN
Lexington, KY

Eastern Ring-Necked Snake

(for Gurney Norman at Hindman)

Long shadows and light, that place,
patched landscape of windfall, rockface, rattler,
where we threw a branch down on the downhill slant
to sit on. Fire joined us then
for pleasure in our smoking —
small fire, flaring
like the lit wick of a reptile's eyes.
We snaked out talking
from the two far places we were:
tongued county speaking to tongued county,
landscape to landscape,
life to life.

And as you scratched a snake's track
idly on a rock
I watched the copperheads of fallen leaves on logs
lie still on our downward path.

Then return and silence earned,
we stood and started back.
We stepped across a wet patch,
and in a half-filled footprint
saw the ring-necked snake,
no longer than a handspan,
its back coal-dark,
its belly smooth and pale, a root.

A root:
I named it,
witnessed how the first I'd ever caught
way up in Ohio
was that kind.

We admired it,
each and each,
then let it go.

But we'd had proof
of all we'd talked about up there,
of a world that's common, shared,
and in the ring-necked snake
a name to give a piece of it
that lives.

Quiet, we lingered in familiar light
to see it moving easily away,
deep into the heartrock
of that homeplace
we both were born to grow to.

RICHARD HAGUE
Cincinnati, OH

———

Hindman, Kentucky

My father, Cortez Day, was born and grew up about five miles from Hindman. When he was a boy, he told me he was lucky to be taken in as a live-in pupil at the Settlement School, where he was given the beginnings of his education. In the mid-1950's, he and I came through Hindman on our way to his half-sister's funeral in Pikeville, and he showed me the Settlement School, including the two-story dormitory standing near the road. In that dormitory, he said, the boys were assigned, two at a time, to start the early-morning fire in the stone fireplace. While taking his turn one cold winter morning, he stood too close to the flames, and his nightshirt blazed up. Instinctively, he ran. His fire-building companion tackled him and smothered the flames, but not before he'd been burned on one thigh, around his torso, and across his back. That explained the scarred flesh I had seen every time he removed his shirt.

In July of 1980 I happened across an announcement for the Appalachian Writers Workshop. Cortez Day had died three years before. Living in Arcata, California, on not a lot of money, I would find it a hardship to get to Hindman, but I had to do it, whatever the cost. So I flew to Lexington by way of San Francisco and Atlanta, then took the bus to Hazard where someone (I think Jim Phelps) met me with a car.

The staff of the Workshop, the other participants, the classes, the readings, the meals, the storytelling sessions on the porch — the contours of the old hills laying shadows on the hollows — met needs of mine so deep I hadn't known I had them. For me, the son of an Appalachian father, the week made for a very rich experience.

Not least was that the dormitory by the road had burned down, leaving only the fireplace with a stub of the chimney, where Cortez Day, some sixty-five years earlier, might have died in his flaming nightshirt.

RICHARD CORTEZ DAY
Arcata, CA

Shared Memories

Just as Dylan Thomas remembered Christmases
overlapping in his native Wales, Appalachian
Writers at Hindman remember seasons of brilliant
flowers, evening readings, uplifting classes.

They see and hear James Still hosting at his cabin,
have the joy of washing dishes with Lee Smith —
or Barbara Smith, Denise Giardina or Robert Morgan.

They perceive the earnestness of Jim Wayne Miller
sharing the gold and silver of regional literature
and the doctoral seriousness as he dissects a poem.

Mingling of the prestigious with the ordinary, with
recognition that none are ordinary. Encouragement,
not competition. A reverent place with history.

Kentucky-made art, friendly organizers, expertise.
George Brosi's book display, George Ella Lyon's
smile, activist discussions, and blossoming flowers.

MARY LUCILLE DeBARRY
Morgantown, WV

In 1996 my daughter Lisa Kaplan, from Lexington, Kentucky, called me in Chicago.

"Mom, you've got to go to Hindman for the Appalachian Writers Workshop."

"Appalachian who, what is it?" I said.

"I'm going and I want you to go with me. There's a richness in Appalachian literature that will blow your mind."

On the basis of that conversation and trust in Lisa I accompanied her. Besides affirming and preserving the importance of Nature, I found a folk poetry that resonated in me; storytellers who were value-oriented: Jim Wayne Miller, Chappell, Morgan; I discovered Lee Smith, Chris Holbrook, my two workshop writers. I'm forever grateful to Lisa and to Hindman Settlement School....

FRAN KAPLAN
Rancho Mirage, CA

I came to Hindman after my first year of college. Having grown up in the gentle, though formidable, hills of the Ohio Valley, Hindman's landscape charged my imagination and intimidated my senses. I remember the sun escaping behind the mountains, that purple aura of late afternoon when the air gets a little colder and the mountains begin to stick their dark angles into the twilight. The lights come on in town, cars speed by along unknown routes. One night, between dinner and the reading, I walked out to call my girlfriend from the payphone at the convenience store. There was no way to communicate the feeling of being down in Hindman, under those mountains. Just a breathless, lucky feeling.

Those few days at the Workshop were my first mature experience with the power of place, and its essential link to poetry. The poetry, prose and storytelling I heard at Hindman left such an impact because it aimed for the praise and preservation of a landscape and a way of life, to speak clearly, to reach everyone who is listening. I took those lessons home, and ever since have tried my best to stay true to that standard.

A few years after Hindman, I spent a year in Ireland, attending an MA Program in Creative Writing. What amazes me is that our most elemental truths travel so well. Irish poetry is also a poetry of place, and like its Appalachian counterpart, is a poetry of genuine human experience. Although my Irish friends had never seen Troublesome Creek, and had only encountered textbook photos of the Appalachian mountains, they were moved by the pure mastery of James Still's *Wolfpen Poems*. Hearing Mr. Still's work read in an Irish brogue was strange, powerful evidence of how well Hindman's concentration of spirit can travel.

MATTHEW FLUHARTY
Beloit, WI

Night Scene

Sometimes, you find this
spot at night on the dock-like
porch attached to a small house
right by Troublesome. Swollen
by rainwater after the drought,
flowing riplets resemble
a black snake
slithering
through
Hindman
Settlement School.

Rippling scales of water
are back-lit-up by a yellow
streetlight over by the road.
The flashing waves appear as
Fox Fire on a hill or a Caribbean
bay disturbed and flashing.

Beto Cumming
Knoxville, TN

A Banquet Barely Tasted

The wisest man I ever knew — we called him Zadie, born 1903, Minsk,
Belarus — once told me a story of a man on a train going from coast to
coast. The train had no dining car. One stop was planned at a half-way
point. There at trackside, a banquet would await the travelers. Caviar,
goat's cheese, olives, fresh melons, figs and dates, soups hot and cold,
rolls baked in a hickory wood stove, roast duck, sugar-cured ham,
turkey with three kinds of stuffing, sweet potatoes, snap peas, baby
carrots, and on and on through a table laden with hand-cranked ice
cream and prizewinning pumpkin and mince pies. But, there were
rules. The train would stop for only half an hour, and no food could
be brought on board. This, Zadie explained, is an allegory of our lives
here on earth — for those of inquisitive mind.

So...now you know how I felt on the eighteenth of July, 1998. No,
I don't file such data in my mind, but I do have a copy of *The Wolfpen
Notebooks* signed by James Still at the celebration of his 92nd birthday.
All was well with the world that day at Little Carr Creek: Mr. Still in
straw hat surrounded by children; Helen Earp in peach-colored blouse

smiling over a table of books — *River of Earth, Jack Tales,* the *Notebooks;* Kentucky historian, "Timeless Thomas" Clark — wife at his side — beaming with a smile to rival that of former Governor Happy Chandler's. Music filled the air — Lee Sexton on banjo, Ray Slone on fiddle, Jennifer Krieger humming along; and under a walnut tree a fellow pinged out notes on a hammered dulcimer as a little boy, walnut in each hand, watched. I drifted toward the house. The big metal wash tub hanging by the kitchen door was garlanded to the rooftop by Virginia creeper, five leaflet fingers waving on each stem, sparkling in sunlight. A rough-hewn table, an appendage of that old log house, was decked with pottery, and held — right by the door — a clear glass jar of Queen Anne's lace and black-eyed Susans one of which, if I'd been a child, I'd have taken.

Inside were Mason jars of home-canned food, pegs for shirts and coats, a wooden hand-crank telephone, and the simplest necessities for cooking, washing, and shaving, a water pail and dipper, and a flyswatter, bright red with white handle. The bed was spread with a hand-made quilt which I'd have bet money was one of Verna Mae Slone's. At the head of the bed was a large portrait of Mr. Still at ease in his wicker rocking chair, book in lap, staring curiously at his visitor. This chair was the spot I was drawn to. I turned around, and there it stood — empty. There I stole a few moments to sit, pretending — wishing — that I could sit there all day, and another day, or maybe a week — maybe all summer. Around me were shelves of books from floor to ceiling. Books Mr. Still had collected, read, shared. Books on topics as diverse as trees, trails, travels, travails, great thoughts, simple thoughts, struggles, and sayings like those my old Aunt Nell loved and treasured — sayings by people she loved…"he's so slow he could fall out of a tree and never get hurt."

I was sitting at a banquet of the mind. Yet, I had but half an hour.

ROBERT E. FRENCH
Lexington, KY

from Clippings

Knott County in Kentucky was a cool green place, an oasis for me, when I came dried out and deprived of sensory stimuli from the Saudi Arabian desert. The Arabian desert was a hot lunar landscape, a gritty place where sandstorms rolled down on you like brown tidal waves. It was a place where the weather was a cocklebur and where demons of old reputedly had fled after Christianity and Islam had seeped into the dusty towns. Knott County, in contrast, looked like God's country: its vertical landscape covered with verdure looked mighty as if it were being held up to be beheld. I drank its moist air like a fish thrown back into cool water.

The camaraderie at the conference was also refreshing. Every evening the teachers and participants gathered on a cabin porch to sing and play guitars. I sang along unembarrassed by my discordant voice, knowing the more experienced and melodic voices would cover my droning — like in church.

The Appalachian Writers Conference has a way of continuing to influence its attendees. For me, this is noticeable especially in the simple fact that wherever I rove, I encounter other writers I first met there, whether it is George Ella Lyon at a book signing in Lexington, Kentucky, or Lana Witt…living in California, or Linda Parsons reading her poems in West Virginia, or Sharyn McCrumb teaching writing in Paris, France.

So the Hindman workshop is best described by a Biblical phrase used by Ernest Hemingway: it has been and continues to be a "moveable feast for me."

ERIK BUNDY
APO

Pilgrimage

Expose a child to a particular landscape
at his susceptible time and he will
perceive in terms of it until he dies.
— Wallace Stegner

When I was a child I had a recurrent dream. I walked over the crest of
the little moraine that bordered my level northwest Minnesota town.
In the waking world this was a hill scarcely half a city block long and
barely sufficient in slope to carry a sled to its eastern base; where a one-
lane road trailed out of town. In my dream it was the entryway to a
maze of hills seven times its height and steepness. At the bottom of the
waking world hill was a bare, flat field. In my dream world — a house
nestled in a notch between the sheltering breasts of surrounding hills.
When I was 21, I discovered it was a real place

I came to east Kentucky as a work camper in 1964 and returned as
an extension teacher at the Hindman and Pine Mountain Settlement
Schools from 1965 to 1970.... My work life took me daily to various
creek-side communities in all parts of the county. I was overpowered
by images and sounds: the naked backbones of the winter hills, the
clop of the mule's feet on Highway 160 on its way to the spring fields,
the view of fog rising from the August hills, the leathery feel of Rhodo-
dendron leaves, the dopdopdop of branches trickling water out of
hillsides onto the shale below, the haunting echo of lined-out hymns
heard from a quarter-mile away around a curve from the graveyard,
the smell of pinto beans simmering on Warm-Morning stoves or of
coal smoke lurking in the winter air. And the language. Above all, the
language. I was in love with language and place. The stories I heard and
lived, are the most vivid in my memory. The language in which I heard
them still rises in my mind. Some writers, even some of my mentors,
call this "material."

But I came from somewhere else. And I left. And I think that making off with someone else's story is appropriation....

When I returned to Hindman to attend the writers workshop after

30 years' absence, I was more than a student — I was a pilgrim. I needed to explore my Kentucky-grounding in the context of my writing, which was then an emerging endeavor in my life. I needed to grapple with this issue of appropriation and I needed to hear the live voices of contemporary Appalachian writers. I came to listen. What I found was a tightly-knit group of articulate writers, many of whom already knew each other, a community of regional artists working to express universal truths in a contemporary voice.

My experience at the Hindman Writers workshop was probably different from that of many who've attended the workshop over the years, because it was colored by my history with the school. That's why I came there — not someplace else. It was a comforting experience to sleep in the very room I'd slept in the old "Hospital" building the first summer I'd been at the school; to slip up the hollow and find hemlocks, pinesap, and honeysuckle in the same old places. But the epiphany there was not about comfort and place. It was discovering that one of my fellow writers was a woman I'd last seen as an 8th grade student in the one room Elmrock School. It was the high level of craft and universal subject matter in the poetry that emerged from Kathryn Byer's poetry class. It was the sense that I wasn't here for nostalgia, but to "go to school" for a week.

We live in an eclectic age of exiles, travelers, and refugees. That clouds the issue of appropriation of geographically based material. But it doesn't cloud good faith between people. There are true stories I will never tell. Being in that community of writers helped me accept the fact even though I'm not an "Appalachian writer," I am a writer whose life, ideas and sensibilities were sculpted by my brief years in that place. I may write about Midwestern rural life, or life in the city village, but Knott County, Kentucky will always be a touchstone for whatever I write, simply because it was and is the touchstone for my life.

NANCY SATHER
Minneapolis, MN

Where It's At

We are wide-ranging writers, but referring to the Hindman Settlement School brings out a peculiar pile of expressions. We say Hindman when we mean the annual Appalachian Writers Workshop. We say *at* Hindman when we mean attending the writer's conference. We say *during* Hindman, as in "One thing you can count on is the feeling that you could NOT stand to have missed whatever it was that was said or read during Hindman." We remember our writing life *before* Hindman, and we can write reams about all that comes *after* Hindman, but the main thing is that *before, during, and after* there are essential stories "*of* and *at*," not to mention the many "*comes from*."

The reason we return to Hindman is that this wordly place is also a connecting place. For me, one treasured consequence has been the writers group I am part of, which took root at Hindman. I can't imagine my life as an artist without it.

However, the actual Hindman is merely a town, and the writer's conference is merely a week. The hanging bridge is just a way to get over Troublesome, and the stonewall that used to gather us like weeds was a way to get over any reluctance or shyness. The years of intense sweating, before the advent of air conditioning in the Stone Building, were just a consequence of summer in the mountains, and those quilts on the wall hang as art, not to torture us with visions of cool nights.

But don't let anyone dare say that this anthology is just a book!

ANN W. OLSON
Olive Hill, KY

The World Is a Wheel

Hindman in August is green and filled with noises — cicadas sawing afternoon heat, the rise and fall of voices in classes and at meals, the drone of readings, the two-beat song of katydids answering tree to tree in darkness, the minor harmonies of mountain music pouring off porches and down the hillsides.

It used to be a lot louder: fans whirring, coal trucks echoing off the sheer rock of the cut-through for the two-lane to Carr, dishes banging in the steel sinks. And it was HOT. You would almost swear you could hear people sweating! And always there was an intensity to all this sound — as if you were at the center of something.

In the basement of the Knott County Public Library, in those old loud days, I first heard the gospel of Appalachian literature eloquently propounded by Jim Wayne Miller above the rattle of fans and the clatter of coal trucks passing on the road above the windows. We sat in folding chairs around the room's edge, pinned by Jim Wayne's piercing eyes and sonorous voice as he put a regional literature I knew almost nothing of into a worldwide context. He had read deeply and broadly and urged us all to do the same. He was fond of quoting Saul Bellow: "A writer is a reader who's been moved to emulation." In the next breath he was quoting Sut Lovingood.

Thus, we came to recognize Sut and Saul as part of our literary family, as Jack Higgs would later make Northrup Frye one of our relations in his lectures in the Great Hall of the May Stone Building. By that time, air conditioning had come to the workshop, and it was much easier to hear the finer points of how our writing connected to the Greeks and Classical literature. We were cooler as we burst into laughter at Jack Higgs' rapier wit, though Jack himself would work up a sweat and made a habit of fanning himself.

Under the spell of Danny Marion's poems and in his gentle teaching,

I felt the Chinese poet awakening — Li Po and Tu Fu his grandfathers, and my own. In George Ella's poetry and fiction I felt Virginia Woolf and Mamaw, two strong and equal foremothers. In conference with Robert Morgan, I was directed to Thomas Hardy's poems as models, brought to ponder formal poetry, a place where many mountain writers start.

When I first met Will, my Floyd County, Kentucky husband, he told me that "the world is a wheel and Prestonsburg is the hub." I laughed at, but loved, his sense of home, his passion for the place from which he'd come.

I discovered a literary world at the Appalachian Writers Workshop, a generous universe. Not a native Appalachian or even a native born Kentuckian, here I felt myself become myself, surrounded by a family in a place where tradition and new voices are equally celebrated. At the Forks of Troublesome, no writer, no matter where she was from, was seen as a "brought-on" How can anyone be "from away," when you are sitting at the hub?

LEATHA KENDRICK
East Point, KY

"Work on creating a sense of place."
And the mountains.
The trees.
The rocks.
The dirt.
The streams.
All listened in.
They knew, they understood, it was
Clear to them what he meant.
"Write about us," they screamed,
"But give us a sense of place."
"Peel back what you see,
And show us what you feel."
The more he spoke, the more
Potential my writing absorbed,
And suddenly I needed my pen.

DAISY LISENBEE WHITE
Monticello, KY

X

LEAVING

Hindman Appalachian Writers Workshop

May the circle never be broken.

Thank you Mike Mullins and all the staff who year after year orchestrate, administrate, bring together, and feed writers.

Thank you Sharyn McCrumb for saying that to be a successful published writer it does no good to hide one's manuscript under the mattress — or words to that effect.

Thank you George Ella Lyon for critiquing one of my stories and sharing your experiences and expertise and giving me hope.

Thank you Kathy Combs and Kitty Lagorio, good friends, for dragging me up the Hill, sweating in the humidity, the heat, and other things, to the men's dorm to invite a lonesome poet to a party.

Thank you Hindman for being the refuge where I met my husband: Philip St. Clair.

Thank you for Appalachian music makers: hammered dulcimers, guitars, and song.

Thank you for rocking chairs on big porches and women of extraordinary words.

Thank you for Jim Wayne Miller and all the other teachers, poets, writers, and friends who join together in a dining hall full of talk and food and fellowship.

May the circle never be broken.

CHRISTINA ST. CLAIR
Rush, KY

Workshop

On the return from Hindman
Words upon words spun in my head
My heart felt soft and rested
Songs still cling to remembering
Of gaiety and unrestrained laughter
My heart warmed and renewed
As I head home from Hindman.

RICHARD D. GARDNER
Morehead, KY

Mountains Call to the Soul

I attended several Appalachian Writers Workshops at Hindman in the 1980's as a student, and taught a couple of nonfiction courses a decade later. Those classes became stepping stones in my writing career. Being at Hindman was almost as good as being home, surrounded by the mountains.

There is no place in the world where I would rather spend a year or a lifetime than in the mountains of Kentucky. It is not fantasy for I lived twenty-nine years in the Kentucky hills, during and after World War II.

Early in my life, I heard the mountains' call even before thinking, before writing. Soon I realized not all people in my world heard the call, but I recognized those who did; they told me about things past as well as things yet to come. They spoke words of joy and sorrow, of contentment and pain, of growing times and times of standing still.

They talked about faithful people who stayed when others made their escape and others who left without warning. Certain people always heard and understood the call and respected the seasons.

When the mountains spoke, my soul knew I was destined to hear them forever, no matter how far I might wander from home. Sometimes it would be just a whisper. Other times the voice came loud as rolling thunder. It came early in the morning when the sun first glinted over a ridge. It came at midday when the sun shone straight down leaving no shadows. The voice rang clear when white mist covered the hills on mornings when it had rained the night before. In the evenings the sound was muted calling us home. Longing for home is one of the most deeply ingrained instincts we mountain people possess. The mind may be cloudy and reasoning powers gone, but still the heart longs for home.

As a little child I was full of light and the clearest vision. I craved to put words together in fresh ways. Wrote poems like square soldiers on a page. I wrote verses like high clouds before it begins to rain. I thought of poetry as water in my existence....

Sad to say while I was growing up in this rich heritage, I developed blind spots. I listened to and tried to emulate educated people from outside the area. I came to believe in them and I worked hard to learn as much as I could about their way of life.

I came to the writers workshops at Hindman Settlement School hoping to learn how to write in a way that would please the outside world. The workshops instead gave me the courage to write about what I knew best — people, places, social actions, and nature.

What it took me such a long time to realize was that I had it all right here in my heart and soul. I didn't need the college education, which became an obsession until I obtained one, to learn how to write. The mountains nurtured me and taught me just about everything I needed to know. My people taught me the rest.

SIDNEY SAYLOR FARR
Berea, KY

Wild Magnolias

I. FOLK

"Community, not competition," so I've heard.
I am, as my great-grandmother used to put it,
juberous, but there it is, waiting, over a wooden bridge,
on the far side of Troublesome Creek. High-summer season,
wild magnolia bloom. For five days I almost belong.

There's Ron with his pipe smoke and Galway tales,
Dana and Rita, Eddy and Laura reading their graceful verse.
There's Phyllis presenting her PIWASH essay, claiming West Virginians
are Yankees! "Madam," I intone, pulling about me the gray wool
of my last life, "We're all Southerners in Summers County,"
then add her to my short list of much-loved Northerners.
There's Marie, slipping a teaspoon of illegal bourbon into her Coke.
Now I know Blanche DuBois proclaimed that "a shot never does a Coke
any harm!" but a teaspoon? "Why bother?" I quiz her.
"That's what my husband says!" she replies, sipping daintily,
so I christen her Mizz Bibulosity, tap her glass with mine,
then slip onto the porch to light a cigar and suck down my Dickel straight.

2. FEASTS

Knott's dry, I'd heard, and by God, it is.
In the local convenience store, I can't even find that fizzy amber water
that passes for beer in most of America. Imagine, if you will,
a thirsty crew of Southern writers, mountain writers, with only
sulfur water and lemonade to drink, and you'll understand prayer,
you'll comprehend canonization, how cross-the-county-line smugglers
    evolve into saints.
The cooks of Hindman Settlement School are angelic already,
setting out spreads worthy of the hillbilly afterlife, the down-home

toothsomes my grandmother used to make. Fried chicken, smoky
brown beans, cornbread, potato salad, turnip greens. And pies, pies, the
simplest happiness: apple, cherry, salacious coconut cream.

Then there's that verboten feast denied the tongue,
which only shy eyes can stroke. Suddenly that grad student sleeping
just down the hall makes me wish I worked in silver nitrate, not syllables,
makes me wish that words could carve solids like sculptors,
could recreate, possess, perpetuate the baby face, the short brown beard,
baggy T-shirt falling off a shelf of pecs. Daybreak in the men's dorm,
he stands yawning, bare-chested and barefoot, in the tousled luck
of morning light. How I envy the sun its liberties, its clover-honeyed hunger
lapping a torso lightly muscled, the moss-swirl of nipple-fur, that ridge
of belly hair descending. Hungry celibate, I stare, then look politely away,
edging along the shaky high wire between subcultures.

3. FOREST

Last evening at Hindman, and over the valley
a storm sweeps in, breaking weeks of drought.
We gather on the hillside porch, where someone lights candles,
someone tunes a guitar and begins to play "The Water is Wide."
Our voices join with theirs, generations nameless, long dead,
singing "love is gentle, and love can be so kind,
the reddest rose when first it's new." Night falls with the rain,
rain driving down hard, filling the withered creek.
None of us has wings, and our song is ending now,
but the storm continues past us. We sit silent
in the welcome sound of it, the drumming on roofs,
the dripping off leaves and eaves. About us,
the trees steam, growing vague with mist,
wild magnolia blossoms gleam like faces in the forest-dark.

JEFF MANN
Blacksburg, VA

from Hindman Homegoing

At my grandmother's funeral in 1994, the sermon was titled "Home-going." I knew nothing of her new home, only that she had left her earthly ground and body for the house of all good and generous souls, a place that may exist both nowhere and everywhere. I knew only that she was gone from me, this woman who was my safe haven in a difficult and unsettling childhood, whose rooms and yard I still wander in my dreams. Despite my grief, the idea of homegoing intrigued me — what definite, conscious action it implies, far more than merely homecoming. What a powerful home it must be to draw us, for just as we mindfully go there, the place itself calls.

And so it is with Hindman. We travel from all parts to attend the annual writers workshop — from the Carolinas, Tennessee, Virginia and West by God, Ohio, California, and points between. Just as we are driven to mold our thoughts and longings into stories, poems, and essays, we head out every summer for Hindman, beckoned by the homing signal of community, kindred minds and hearts, respect for words and for those who unendingly fill blank pages with one, then another, and another.

So many comings and goings to remember. The first time I drove to the workshop, eight or nine years ago, I made a wrong turn in Hazard. Soon I was completely lost. The hairpin curves wound me deeper into the black mouth of coal country, but each time I stopped to ask directions at a little market or gas station I was assured, "Keep going, Hindman's on up the road." I kept going then; I keep going now....

Since my first visit to Hindman I have known more firsts than lasts, and what I have learned will not fit in any knapsack or notebook. Still, I carry these lessons with me all year long. I have learned that being an introvert among such grand talkers and spinners is not so terrible. I dearly wish I could hold my own equally in the spoken word as on the page, but a good listener is a rare and important thing. With workshops all day and readings every afternoon and evening, I have learned to pace myself and, hard as it is to miss a speaker I admire, take a nap when exhaustion overwhelms me. (Forgive me, Bobbie Ann, for leaving your session so abruptly. I preferred rudeness over the *thud* I would have made falling out of my chair.) I have learned to pack lightly and let the July heat drench me, for it is only the excellent sweat of word-play and story weave, the grease of our ink and memory engines pumping away. I have learned that, in a country of prolific graduate programs pitting student against student and shredding their words to pieces, writers of all genres can come together in one humble place and leave their fiefdoms and competitive games behind. How refreshing, how safe this haven in a difficult and unsettling world. Just as we long for a change in season, for gray winter to pass on and the violets to show their faces once more, we who have been "Hindmanized" begin counting down the months, then the weeks until our return, this yearly ritual planted so deep in us now. Again we enter this house of good and generous souls, our long-awaited homegoing.

LINDA PARSONS MARION
Knoxville, TN

Hindman Litany

I praise the Rose of Sharon Tree halfway up the hill
        to my home for a week
I praise the friends I meet there who are my friends still
I praise the poems we read by Troublesome Creek
I praise its own buoyant brown babble

I praise footsprung paths that loop and cross, drawing
        us in, come dawn, come dark
I praise the dining room where dialogue, made-from-scratch,
        home-cooked in heart juices, is food
        for the thoughtful hungry
I praise bright rhythm of fiddle, cry of guitar, old hymns,
        modern bars beating out a circle of sound where
        our new-found inspiration lights up the night

I praise knotty-pine verse, copperhead prose,
        clapboard sonnet, mockingbird ode,
        the authentic thrill of Appalachian fiction
        universally real
I praise heaven's Highlanders — Jim Wayne, Harriette Arnow,
        Mr. Still — all present in what's below:
I praise their good-time laughter continuing in our own,
        their roof-top claps in the din of our applause,
        their voices signals in the August breeze that
        work done here will go out in the world
        to endure, prevail. Defeat defeat.
           Learn, grow.

LLEWELLYN MCKERNAN
Barboursville, WV

from Our Last Night at Hindman

At sundown, an alarm of crows rises from the trees as a red-tailed hawk dives near. Frogs and insects tune evening instruments. Finally, in darkness we say good night. Dory Hudspeth bravely up the hill, flashlight darting. The rest of us to our lower dorms. Packed and ready to depart at dawn, we turn in, until a storm to end all storms shakes the roof and rattles our brains. Suddenly, a man in hip boots warns of rising water —Troublesome Creek living up to its name.

In pajamas and slippers we follow him out into the deluge...the creek now creeping toward us, endangering our cars. Debris rushes by. Lights twinkle in windows as people rouse to prepare for flood. After moving vehicles to higher ground, we wipe down benches and folding chairs, settle in on the dorm porch to see what comes next. Chipper and excited, we ignore odd attire, bad hair days turned to nightmares. Sleep seems unlikely.

Thunder rumbles in the hills. Lightning flashes, but no more rain. Are we glad or not? This is the most excitement we've had since Celeste Keyes lost the brakes on her car and barreled down the hill like Mario Andretti, swooping around the dorm and dining hall before sailing into the green bank. Hindman boring? Never!

CATHY LENTES
Middleport, OH

Baptism

Raindrops fall
as I enter the mountains.
They are cleansing me
from the sin
that doth so easily beset us.

I shut my eyes
drinking in the voices
of rank strangers
I've known from the womb.
Ancient tones mingle
with fresh laughter
and echo back
from jagged hillsides.
My senses ripple
like a tiny stone
tossed
on the surface of my soul.

Moments later
rain falls again
as I drift westward
gasping for air
resurrected to live
at last
and forever.

DAVID BAXTER
Smiths Grove, KY

Postcards from Hindman

◄§► Angie DeBord, long black hair going every whichaway as she turns into somebody else before our very eyes, peeking down through the boards in the porch to find the stubborn memories lodged beneath.

◄§► Jack Higgs reared back and laughing....

◄§► Mr. Still's sharp brown eyes, his hat, his big new car, his wonderful stories which always end with a self-deprecating, "But no matter."

◄§► Jonathan Greene's sardonic grin,

◄§► George Brosi's dandelion hair,

◄§► Al Stewart's little mischievous smile,

◄§► Dana's shiny tights,

◄§► Ed's gold cowboy boots....

◄§► The time I told a student in class that her story was not realistic, that nobody would carry their mama's ashes around in the trunk of their car, and she jumped up and ran out to her car to get them, in a mason jar....

◄§► Leatha reads a poem which rings like a bell in the hushed hall....

◄§► Mike, the drill sergeant, keeps us in line, or tries to....

◄§► Mary Hodges puts her bonnet on, cocks her head, and starts in: "Why, everybody just calls me Ida Mae...."

◄§► In the kitchen, Sharyn McCrumb and I imagine a perfect murder, done with the materials at hand: "An injection of mayonnaise," she finally decides, "but it's got to be Hellman's...."

◄§► A clutch of women wade in the creek after dinner, skirts lifted, cooling off....

◦§◦ Rita closes her eyes and leans into a song…Silas clogs…Lisa and Rae wail out on "Goodbye Earl"…while Betty Smith's high sweet voice takes us back, back, back up the hollers, home…no matter where we're from.

◦§◦ Smoke from Jim Wayne's cigarette yet lingers in the air, of an evening, on the porch.…

◦§◦ Loyal Jones tells about the fellers down in front of the courthouse discussing religion: "Do you believe in infant baptism?" asks one. "Believe in it?!" repeats his buddy. "Why hell, I've seen it done!"

◦§◦ Chris Holbrook gets right down to it, just in case anybody is having too much fun, just in case anybody is ever in any danger of forgetting for a minute how serious, how very important, all this is — for it is here, at Hindman, in the telling of stories and poems that we discover again and again who we are, what matters, what we should do.…

As I walk my illegal dog before breakfast, I pause on the bridge to look all around at the misty, sleeping Settlement School — can it really be 25 years ago that Mike called me up to say, "We're having us a writers conference over here, and you need to come to it." Back then I didn't understand how true that was, but I do now, and I'm still here.

LEE SMITH
Hillsborough, NC

from Stories of the Leaf Writers

It is memory that propels us all back there every August to experience something that cannot be put into words. That is truly the ultimate irony. The one place where so many words have taken flight, where language is the currency, the framing, and the fuel, where people are so enthusiastic about their ideas that they would, as poet George Ella Lyon said, "take leaves off the trees to write on them," defies description on paper.

Rita Quillen
Gate City, VA

A writers' conference is about words. It is also about getting there…paying attention along the way to signs…road signs / signs of life, scribbles in a notebook, a leaf spinning on a branch when there is no wind.

When I think back to my journeys from North Carolina right up to crossing Troublesome Creek, my whole body fills up with movie-screen-sized snapshots that take me straight back to Hindman. But I can't write about them. They're too big and too detailed. You who've been there…you know what I mean.

Louanne Watley
Chapel Hill, NC

INDEX OF AUTHORS